GETTING THERE WITHOUT DRUGS

GETTING THERE WITHOUT DRUGS

Techniques and Theories for the Expansion of Consciousness

BURYL PAYNE

WILDWOOD HOUSE LONDON

First published in Great Britain 1974

Copyright © 1973 Buryl Payne

An Esalen Book

Wildwood House Limited
1 Wardour Street, London W1V 3HE

ISBN Hardback   0 7045 0075 2
       Paperback 0 7045 0077 9

Printed in Great Britain by
Lowe & Brydone (Printers) Ltd, Thetford, Norfolk.

DEDICATED TO THE STUDENTS AT GODDARD COLLEGE
WHO WERE MY TEACHERS
AND THE STUDENTS AT BOSTON UNIVERSITY
WHO WERE MY EDITORS

Reading with acknowledgment is nothing—
doing is everything.
You were born with wings,
why prefer to crawl through life?
Grasp the Joy of Living

THE INVISIBLES

Acknowledgments

Margot Johnson Agency: 'Moment' from *New and Selected Poems* by Howard Nemerov, copyright by the University of Chicargo, 1960.

Alfred A. Knopf, Inc.: from *The Prophet* by Kahlil Gibran. Copyright 1923 by Kahlil Gibran; renewal copyright 1951 by Administrators C.T.A. of Kahlil Gibran Estate and Mary G. Gibran. Reprinted with permission of Alfred A. Knopf, Inc.

The M.I.T. Press: from *Language, Thought, and Reality* by B. L. Whorf.

Pantheon Books, Inc.: from *The Supreme Doctrine* by Hubert Benoit. Copyright 1955 by Pantheon Books, Inc.

Random House, Inc.: from *Selected Poetry of Robinson Jeffers*. Copyright 1935 and renewed 1963 by Donnan Jeffers and Garth Jeffers. Reprinted by permission of Random House, Inc.

Charles E. Tuttle Co., Inc.: from *Zen Flesh, Zen Bones* by Paul Reps

Vedanta Press: from *The Upanishads,* translated by Swami Prabhavananda and Frederick Manchester

Xerox College Publishing: from *The World of Elementary Particles* by Kenneth Ford. © 1963 by Xerox Corporation. All rights reserved.

FOREWORD

The view of the world inherited from nineteenth-century science has led us astray. This science concentrated primarily on "things" of the world, neglecting the experiencers of those things, and led us to ignore any processes or events which could not be subjected to the rules of "thing" manipulation or described by the purely rational laws of logic. Aspects of reality which did not fit into the scheme devised for "things" were either evaluated as nonscientific and not worthy of study, or force-fitted into a logical scheme. As a consequence, we have gradually developed an artificial reality which excludes a great portion of the universe. We have also come, as a culture, to treating people like things and manipulating them as though they were objects—so many tin soldiers and mechanical clerks—and this subtle and pervasive philosophy of squeezing everything into rational schemes has actually made people more thinglike, more robotized and dehumanized.

Although there are many who firmly believe that man functions as a rigidly determined machine and that no progress is possible, such a position of despair leads nowhere. Whatever the actual truth, the only sensible course to take is the opposite; man is more than a machine, more than an animal. He has some choice in determining the course of his development in life as well as some power in influencing the society around him.

Several erroneous assumptions in nineteenth-century science have pushed our cultural philosophy in the direction of rational mechanical thinking. Some of these are:

1. That all known forms of energy have been discovered.
2. That our ordinary consciousness of space and time is necessarily the correct view.
3. That men live as separate and autonomous individuals.
4. That the essence of a man rigidly depends upon the existence of his physical body.

Modern twentieth-century science has formulated different ways of looking at the universe which in turn support a different conception of man. Fortunately, a counterrevolution is now taking place and it overlaps in many ways with this modern view of man. This book is part of that counterrevolution. It is based on the notion that a different state of being is possible for man—that he is not just a "thing" of the world, but potentially much more. Man *can* free himself from the entanglements of technocratic society. He does not have to think and behave like a machine. He need not feel himself alienated and alone in a universe he never made. Man can see his unification with all other men and living creatures, with his planet as a whole, and in a sense can transcend even the limitations of space and time. He has the power.

This view of man does not oppose the findings of twentieth-century science. While some of the most recent advances in science support this view, there remains, however, a big gap between a few tidbits of scientific knowledge and practical techniques which may help men realize their ultimate potential.

Our present state of knowledge about man's potential is at about the same level as that of man's first attempt, two hundred years ago, to understand the "mysterious" phenomena of electricity, forces which we now control with the flick of a switch, and which are available to nearly every man, not to just a few isolated scientists.

Today we have only the weakest and scantiest knowledge of extrasensory perception, mental telepathy, precognition, out-of-body travel, or mystical states of awareness. But who knows what tomorrow's knowledge will bring? I think science is on the verge of discovering a new type of energy which may be as useful to the development of men's lives as electricity has been to the development of men's machines. This type of energy may be manifest now, but only in the strange and feeble way that electricity and magnetism were known before the nineteenth century.

Mystical experiences may relate to the production of this type of energy. Such experiences play an integral part in many men's lives, although few men may recognize them as such. You've probably had an experience that was out of the ordinary or you wouldn't be reading this book. Every man occasionally catches a glimpse of the meaning of his life in relationship to the universe, and pauses—momentarily uplifted and touched at a deeper level —before returning once more to his everyday state. We may not know how to fit mystical experiences into our lives, but we are forced to admit that such experiences have profoundly influenced the conduct of many persons.

Some of the greatest intellectual and artistic figures were intimately familiar with mystical experiences; indeed, such experiences seemed to be major influences in their lives. Albert Einstein once said: "The most beautiful emotion we can experience is the mystical. It is the source of all true art and science. He to whom this emotion is strange, who can no longer wonder and stand in rapt awe, is as good as dead."

Mystical experiences have been sought by people of all cultures and ages, from the Egyptian priests to the African bushmen, from the Tibetan lamas to the American Indians. Techniques have ranged from drug-taking to fasting, from meditating quietly to dancing wildly until exhausted. Now, however, more men than ever before are seeking such experiences, attempting to understand them, and bring them under control.

I am one of these men and it is my hypothesis that mystical experiences are not supernatural or surreal, but aspects of consciousness which we ordinarily do not use. If we could alter or expand our ordinary state of consciousness, we would see that mystical experiences are perfectly natural views of the universe; they represent a psychological destination, not a physical one, a different way of being in the world.

In the last few years, marijuana, LSD, mescaline, and other psychedelic drugs have provided large numbers of persons with mystical-like experiences. The use of these drugs may expand consciousness, but drugs may also harm the persons taking them. Hospitals have had to deal with increasing numbers of people who have had bad trips, who have "flipped-out," "cracked-up," "blown their minds," or otherwise failed to adjust to the alterations and disturbances produced by some of the more powerful psychedelic substances.

I have observed that psychedelic drugs may amplify personality defects. Furthermore, many persons simply cannot handle the new state of consciousness suddenly thrust upon them by taking drugs. The phrases "blow your mind" or "bend your mind" aptly describe the condition of being overwhelmed or overloaded with awareness before one can readily assimilate or comprehend it.

Achieving a more conscious state requires a certain kind of psychological health and strength. One must be what I call "grounded" in this normal state of consciousness if one is to "get there" and stay there or return at will. It is necessary to know "where one is at," as they say, to be able to move comfortably here and now in this world and establish solid ties with the earth of sun, sand, water, trees, and, especially, other people.

All of this takes living and working; there is no shortcut, no instant satori. But, it is not wearisome work, it is not a grinding, joyless discipline. The path is light and rewards follow; one must only make the effort to move.

This book has grown organically from my life's work and my teaching. Originally, I studied physics and mathematics, but as I realized the limitations of physics, I moved into psychology. Alfred Korzybski's writings showed me how the formulations of modern science could be useful in helping people develop more fully as human beings. When I came upon Zen and other Eastern psychologies and religions I saw connections between them and modern twentieth-century science. When I began to teach, I began to learn. When I began to write, I began to understand. In this book I attempt to unite the wisdom of the Eastern teachers with the formulations of modern science since, as I see it, each side is heading toward some of the same goals. I have not been able completely to unite these views with diagrams or equations, but perhaps you will be able to make the leap on your own.

I designed the exercises, ideas, and experiments in this book to help a person in his evolutionary or spiritual growth toward enlightenment, Buddhahood, awakening, satori, or whatever you choose to name it. You may also find them just as useful in the ordinary course of your everyday life.

I suggest that you read this book not to find out what its conclusions are, but to treat it as a workbook to be read and used slowly.

There is no magic ending to be found in my book, only in the efforts you make and the work you do. I designed the exercises so that each one leads to the next wherever possible, and so that each chapter builds upon the one before it. If you merely skim the text, it may seem like so many empty words and dry phrases, but if you work on the exercises, even a little, a meaning will emerge for you.

Readers who have taken psychedelic drugs or are planning to take them may find that the exercises and ideas in this book will make their experiences more meaningful. Or that they will be a little less likely to take a bad trip.

I have given some rationale and some theory for many of the exercises, based upon notions from physics, information theory, biology, and neurology. For some of the exercises I have no real theory or complete understanding. Some of the exercises were invented or discovered by myself and my students in the course of various seminars and workshops. Others were culled from the references listed at the end of the book* or from various teachers under whom I have worked. I have only included in this book those exercises that were of value to me personally. There are many other exercises and techniques I have found valuable, but they are either too complicated to be described in words, or must be adapted to each individual for the best results.

Since I wrote this book as much for myself as for the reader, I make no claim to be a master of any sort, merely another interested seeker on a path. Ultimately, you are the master; the gains you derive from this book will be based entirely on your initiative and your needs of the moment. Pick and choose as you will.

Life offers very rich experiences, and for us lucky ones it can be much richer. I cannot give my riches to you, but they are there for your taking.

* The additional references begin on page 203.

Ryokan, a Zen master, lived the simplest kind of life in a little hut at the foot of a mountain. One evening, a thief visited the hut to discover there was nothing in it to steal. Ryokan returned and caught him. "You may have come a long way to visit me," he told the prowler, "and you should not return empty-handed. Please take my clothes as a gift." The thief was bewildered. He took the clothes and slunk away. Ryokan sat naked, watching the moon. "Poor fellow," he mused, "I wish I could give him this beautiful moon."

—*Zen Flesh, Zen Bones*

CONTENTS

1 OPENING GATEWAYS

There are many paths to enlightenment though they all begin and end at the same point. In this section I systematically explore some of the major ones, emphasizing their commonness. Some hard and simple exercises given in each chapter will help you expand your sensory awareness, achieve internal silence, meditate, contact an inner essence, and ultimately a transpersonal self. These exercises are the reason for the book, but they are only gateways; the real exploration is left to you.

Where Are We?

"Cheshire-Puss," she [Alice] began, rather timidly, as she did not at all know whether it would like the name: however, it only grinned a little wider. "Come, it's pleased so far," thought Alice, and she went on. "Would you tell me, please, which way I ought to walk from here?"

"That depends a good deal on where you want to get to," said the Cat.

"I don't much care where———" said Alice.

"Then it doesn't matter which way you go," said the Cat.

"———so long as I get *somewhere,*" Alice added as an explanation.

"Oh, you're sure to do that," said the Cat, "if you only walk long enough."

—LEWIS CARROLL

Man is not just an animal. Nor has he arrived at the culmination of the evolutionary process. According to Pierre Teilhard de Chardin, he is still very primitive and is being pushed whether he likes it or not along the path of further evolution. While many of the world's millions are starving, living in the most bestial conditions, seemingly unaware of their own humanity, with brains bent to tasks no more complex than how to catch a fish, or

3

enhance some simple pleasure, millions of other people are pushing on with all their power to develop, expand, and increase their potential in all areas. Considered as a superorganism in its own right, the race of man has its thinking part and its merely functioning parts. A few beings, pushing ahead, lead and influence the vast majority. A few individuals may evolve into some *higher state,* while most still remain merely men, more or less animal-like in their behavior. Some say that the race of man is doomed to extinction and will be replaced by *Homo superior,* but none can say where or how that will happen or what form he might take.

Homo superior may already be present. There are vast differences in ability among people, and accomplished men seem like supermen when compared to novices in the same field. A few young men can run a mile in less than four minutes, but most can hardly run a mile at all. The majority of the world's population cannot work algebra problems, and the intricate manipulations of tensor calculus or differential geometry seem far above their capabilities. (I myself cannot reproduce the melody of the simplest tune, so those who can recall whole passages of a symphony at a single hearing are supermen to me).

These abilities comprise only superficial skills for the most part, but other areas of development exist in which the differences between men are just as great and perhaps more important. One of the most significant differences lies in the development of that subtle phenomenon called consciousness. Our bodies have remained about the same for eons but our use of the cortex for self-awareness and reflective thought has altered tremendously. According to Teilhard, evolution has always been in the direction of increasing consciousness, not simply toward a change of physical form. He considers consciousness a motive force of evolution. It is not something added to the universe any more than a charge is something added to an electron. Rather, consciousness entails the unfolding, the manifesting of something that has always remained hidden. The next step in evolution will not be a step at all, but a gradual flowering of even greater consciousness.

Throughout history certain individuals have seemed to possess more consciousness than those around them: individuals born ahead of their time—great scientists, artists, saints, mystics, or humanitarians—who served as models for other men and women. There have always been people in the past who used their mental capacities more fully than their contemporaries, but today there are more people intent on developing their brain power than at any other time.

More scientists are alive now, and also more artists, musicians, and other intellectuals than ever before. Man's capacity to experience and understand all forms of science, of art, and of his own psychic functioning may not have changed, but his use of that capacity has increased tremendously in the past hundred years.

The advent of communications media such as radio, television, recordings, photographs, books, newspapers, instant copiers, etc., has exponentially increased the information flow from one brain to another. Indeed, most of us are overwhelmed by this flood of information and find that there is more knowledge available in every field of human functioning than we can ever hope to assimilate. But the information itself has little to do with the essential difference, which is becoming ever more apparent. People are trying to awaken, to become more conscious of what they are and how they operate as functioning organisms, and are aware for the first time that the more their consciousness develops, the greater their freedom will be.

Thousands of people, especially in the United States, are now on what is called a "spiritual growth trip." They are flocking to Yogis, Zen masters, and gurus of all types trying to find some secret, or magic formula of meditation; some esoteric self-discipline which will enable them to awaken their consciousness or to develop some occult or psychic powers.

In the last century, Sigmund Freud pioneered in helping man discover his unconscious. Modern psychotherapists, psychiatrists, and psychologists continue his work at an ever-increasing pace. Their aim is to make the unconscious conscious, for if what is unconscious affects our choices, then our alternatives may be limited, our freedom constricted, and our health impaired. This is very fine work and millions of people have been helped by it, either directly by a teacher or psychiatrist, or indirectly via the general cultural milieu.

But Freud didn't go far enough; and we are now ready for the next step. He assumed that there was an unconscious, but more accurately we should say that there exist at least two unconscious minds or functions—a lower unconscious and a higher unconscious. The lower unconscious strait-jackets us, makes us rigid and unadaptable to present, ever-changing circumstances. If we react to all women the way we reacted to our mother, or if we continue to punish ourselves for innocent childhood actions, we are victims of our mechanistic lower unconscious. The lower unconscious seems to think literally, in two-valued categories of yes or no, good or bad, love or hate, with no time-indexing or situation-indexing. For instance, if a child is told that he is dumb in arithmetic, he may come to believe that he is completely dumb for all time and in all situations. He becomes a victim of his mechanistic, lower unconscious mind.

The higher unconscious serves to guide us through the maze of our daily lives. It is the source of our inspiration, our creativity, and our grand intuitive flashes of understanding. Our greatest moments of love, our richest connections with life, flow to and from the higher unconscious. Mystical experiences, flashes of telepathy, clairvoyance, or other paranormal abilities all seem to be functions of this higher mind, and there are few men who don't make contact with it sometime in their lives.

Ordinarily, though, our contact with the higher unconscious is transitory and feeble. If classical psychotherapy gave us techniques for communicating with our lower unconscious, we now need a more advanced psychotherapy for communicating with our higher unconscious. To develop our human potential to the fullest, we must either find a spiritual leader or guru (that is, a superpsychotherapist) or attempt to pull ourselves up by our own stumbling efforts. The connection of man's normal consciousness with these other forms of consciousness—or the expansion of normal consciousness to include them—seems to be one of man's major evolutionary tasks, transcending all other problems of maturation and development. Each man, starting at his own level, may have a different pathway. Each may choose to lie in idleness and sleep beside the trail or to keep on working his way along it, struggling to make progress. Life is a kind of proving ground for those who want to better themselves—in intellectual ability, in the ability to feel, to move, to play, to help themselves or others, to develop their psychic powers, or higher consciousness. Man's real life lies in the development of his consciousness. He is born into the machinery of his body, and into a given culture; he can't ignore or deny these factors, but he *can* extend the focus of his attention and his efforts far beyond them.

Most men have little control over the circumstances of their lives, but they seldom exercise even what control they have in choosing conditions that will help develop their abilities to the fullest. Unless an individual undertakes special exercises, he will generally lapse into living in certain set patterns, and will remain essentially a complex machine—living, breeding, and functioning in an automatic or unconscious fashion—tragically asleep to his real potential.

This is as true for the highly educated man as for the most humble peasant, for the connections to higher consciousness are not much developed by traditional education.

The whole quest for an expanded consciousness can be pushed outside the range of ordinary life by calling it mysticism, or assuming that a man has to go to a monastary in India or Japan or Afghanistan, live on rice, arise at 4:00 every morning, and spend most of his hours in solitude and chastity. Such a regime may work now and then, but it is not necessary for all. Every minute of every man's life contains opportunities for expanding consciousness, indeed for just being conscious. You need not go anywhere. You can begin right now, right this minute.

Stop reading. Look around you. Where are you? What are you doing? What are you seeing? What are you feeling? What are you thinking? What are the muscles in your body doing? Take all this awareness in. Then continue reading, but try to keep the other things in your consciousness as well.

In order to evolve a man must know where he is now—what he is doing, sensing, feeling, thinking, and how he is grounded to the earth. The path to higher consciousness winds its way through the lower consciousness.

In order for a man to blossom he must be keenly aware of his nature as an animal, rooted to the physical world, to the sun and seas, to the smell of flowers and the touch of trees, to the feel of earth under his feet and the wind in his hair. A man must be firmly grounded in his loves and hates, in his joys and angers. He must know the ache of well-worked muscles and the quiet peace of deep sleep.

He must know and accept the brute within before he can be a man and touch the God within.

> In the pasture of this world, I endlessly push aside the tall grasses in search of the bull.
> Following unnamed rivers, lost upon the interpenetrating paths of distant mountains,
> My strength failing and my vitality exhausted, I cannot find the bull.
> I only hear the locusts chirring through the forest at night.
>
> —Zen Flesh, Zen Bones

9   *Where Are We?*

Sensory Awareness— Expanding Ordinary Consciousness

We are conscious of only a small portion of the larger world which teems around and through us. Although our field of awareness may seem large to us, it is insignificantly minute when compared with what instruments tell us exists beyond the range of our senses. Unperceived radiations and vibrations resonate all about us. Radio waves, infrared rays, microwaves, cosmic rays, ultrasonic waves, ultraviolet rays, and other forms of energy bombard us every instant of our lives. Who can say what messages, what beauty they might convey, if only we could perceive them?

Look at the reproduction of the electromagnetic spectrum on the opposite page, Figure 1. The wave lengths of electromagnetic radiation vary from more than 100 meters to less than 1 trillionth of a meter. We are aware of only the tiny fraction called "visible light" in any detail. All the rest of that spectrum remains invisible to our eyes although our skin can "sense" infrared light as heat, and ultraviolet light as sunburn. In the tiny region between four and seven ten-millionths of a meter in wave length, we can distinguish six major divisions which we name red, orange, yellow, green, blue, and violet. These colors *don't exist in the*

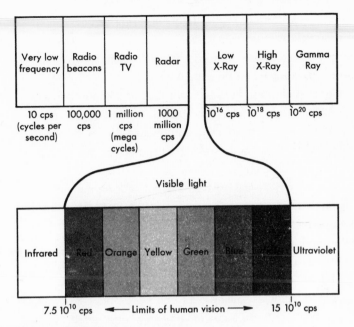

Figure 1. Electromagnetic spectrum.

world—they are simply names for light waves of different energy or frequency. If we could perceive wave-length changes in other portions of the spectrum as sharply as we distinguish them in the region from four to seven ten-millionths, then we would have, say, a color sensation for the waves between eight and nine ten-millionths, a different color for the next set of waves between 1 and 1.1-millionth of a meter, and so on. If we perceived a different color sensation for every band of waves, 1 ten-millionth of a meter wide up to a length of one-thousandth of a meter, that would be over 10,000 more colors! At present, we lump that whole range of energies together under one single term: "infrared" and the infrared is still a very small portion of the total electromagnetic spectrum. Lower frequency light waves such as those used by radio or TV constantly flow around us, unnoticed,

11   *Sensory Awareness—Expanding Ordinary Consciousness*

and harmlessly absorbed. Higher frequency light waves, called x-rays, pass right through our bodies, occasionally destroying a cell but never consciously noticed either (although some people do report sensations when they are X-rayed).

In addition to all these invisible light rays of different energies, there exist thousands of subatomic particles called cosmic rays which pass through us every day, contributing now and then to our aging process by directly striking a cell nucleus but again never observed consciously.

Some of the invisible light waves emanating from humans and other living organisms are seen as "auras." My wife occasionally sees these auras, and I've met others who have too. Most evident around a person who is excited, auras seem to correspond to emotional states and personality traits of each individual. (Perhaps they are overtones or harmonics of extra-visible frequencies spilling over into the visible band width.) Recently, aspects of these auras have been photogaphed by special devices. Pinacyanole bromide filters make it possible for the average person to see some aura effects, but most of us are still blind to them, as well as to the major part of the light spectrum.

We are not quite as restricted in the sound spectrum; we can hear sounds ranging in frequency from 16 to 15,000 cycles per second. The ultrasonic region from 15,000 to over 100,000 cycles per second is insensible to us, although dolphins talk to each other in the 20,000 cycle range, and bats hear up to 70,000 cycles per second. Perhaps living organisms have their sound auras too, though most of us are deaf to them.

While it would be wonderful to expand our vision over even a fraction more of the electromagnetic spectrum to see auras or cosmic ray showers, and hear ultrasonic symphonies, or gaze on the fireworks of cosmic ray showers, we don't even use what minute capacity we have. We tune out perhaps 75 per cent of what lies within our sensory range through our own neglect, lack of interest, or bad habits.

We have eyes, but we do not see; we have ears, but we do not hear; we have the sense of touch but we do not. We go through life as if we were asleep and dreaming, even at high noon. It is as if we were color blind; we take in only shades of black and white, unaware of the richness and color of the sensory world around us. How many of us take the time to look at an ordinary scene, just to enjoy the colors? How many of us remember to take the time to savor a glass of water?

If we were fully aware of the thousands of sensations potentially available to us at any given second, we would be overwhelmed by the variety of sensory input. There is a limit to the rate at which we can handle information, to the number of things we can simultaneously attend to, and the number of ideas we can hold in our heads at the same time. As infants, we are bombarded with thousands of stimuli from every event, every object. Given that we have only a certain capacity for dealing with this input, we may react to the overload either by turning off our awareness or by attempting to increase our ability to handle it. The desire to act with minimum effort usually leads us to cut off as much input as possible. We become selective about what we pay attention to; we turn off what we think is uninteresting or unimportant. If we looked at something once, we don't bother to look a second time—we think we "know" what it is like. After a while such patterns of behavior become habitual; we no longer have conscious control of what we let in and what we block out. More and more we live in a verbal world, as if in a trance; only extreme sensory input jars us awake. People often seek exciting things to do or beautiful places to visit because they have lost the capacity to turn themselves on; they require an external environment strong enough to do it for them. They hope the new environment will be intense enough to break through their canalized perception habits, for they have starved themselves of the food of impressions. Drugs have provided yet another means of breaking through calcified habitual patterns of perception and thinking, but their effect, like that of travel, is only temporary.

Though I can't promise you ways to expand your sensory capacity into the ultraviolet or ultrasonic ranges, I suggest that there is much you can do to broaden your sensory awareness. It is well worth the effort to exercise your brain's "muscles" just as you might exercise your body's muscles.

Expanding sensory awareness largely involves discarding old habits of thinking-perceiving. This requires hard work and probably some discomfort, for old habits, like old clothes, may have become so much a part of you that giving them up hurts a little bit.

In order to "take off" your old habits, you must first identify them and then separate yourself from them; you must recognize that they are not *you*. In the exercises and experiments that follow, try to recognize a mechanical part of you which merely perceives and labels sensations or evaluates situations and events in stereotyped ways. At first this split may seem artificial and arbitrary, but as you work with the exercises, you will see more clearly what is innately yours and what has been acquired from people around you by learning and imitation.

If you wish, modify the specific exercises in this book to fit your individual needs. The important thing is to give the exercises a good try, at least two or three times, and preferably ten or twenty times. Like physical exercises performed to develop muscle, these exercises ought to be done regularly if you want to make progress. There is no short cut and no substitute for persistent daily efforts.

Some people will attempt to decide in advance whether or not the exercise will be of any value or will think they have understood the exercise after reading about it. This kind of priority to verbal levels blocks their progress. Certainly you can make hypotheses about what will happen, and I will try to provide you with a verbal rationale, but ultimately there exists no substitute for your own experiencing.

You will probably work most effectively if you keep a notebook. Write down your reactions to the exercises each time you do them. Writing will help you stay in an observing mode of behavior and shed habits which are not innately yours.

The first set of exercises are designed to help you expand your listening abilities and master the art of achieving "internal silence," a basic first step in "getting there." Here is the first one:

Listen for about thirty seconds. As you listen, write down some of what you hear.

Now look over what you have written. Some typical responses might be : "car going by," "someone typing," "door shutting," or "people talking." Notice the kind of things you have written. Are they names of sounds themselves or are they names of sources of the sounds? We are so accustomed to associating sound with their sources that we do it automatically. Try the exercise again with the aim of studying this automatic reaction.

Listen and write down what you hear. Observe how your process of mentation works. Observe how quickly your mechanical mind categorizes sounds and infers their origin. What happens when an unfamiliar sound is heard? Can you note the searching and struggling to identify its origin?

After you have gotten a sense of this mechanical association process, try to inhibit it. Try the following exercise, as an intermediate step:

Listen for one minute. As you listen write down only the names of sounds. Try to refrain from inferring what is making each

sound. Keep your attention focused on the sound itself. Label the sounds with words that refer strictly to what the sound is like rather than what produces it.

For example: a typewriter makes a clickety-clack sound, a car makes a roaring-hissing-rumbling sound, a door shutting makes a thud sound, etc. Be ingenious and make up your own names for various sounds.

The final step in full listening takes you to where you can eliminate internal verbalizing of any and all kinds. Did you notice during the last exercise how inadequate words or other symbols are for sound sensations? That which cannot be captured by words makes every sound unique and often enjoyable in and of itself. Unfortunately, we usually stop listening when we give the sound a name or identify its origin. We turn off the sensation and substitute the symbol instead. All this happens in an instant without our wishing it or controlling it. This is learned behavior, though, and we can unlearn it with a little practice.

Try to listen for one full minute to the sounds around you without making inferences about the origins of the sounds or labeling them in any way. Try to listen without having any words come into your mind.

This is a key exercise, worth doing many, many times, but it is very difficult. *Do not feel upset or scold yourself if you cannot do it. Be patient and gentle with yourself.* Do not expect 100 percent success on the first try. It may take many tries, much effort, and perhaps more practice of the intermediate steps. In the beginning you may only be able to achieve internal silence for a second or two at a stretch, but gradually your ability will increase. You will begin to expand your "listening consciousness" and turn the world back on.

May you have as much success with this exercise as one of my students who had been trying for a week and suddenly came bursting into my office, eyes flashing with joy, and said: "I listened. For the first time last night, I really listened. It was fantastic."

One related exercise that you might try is to coordinate internal talking with breathing:

> **As you inhale, talk to yourself about what you hear. Label the sounds and/or their origins. As you exhale, babble about anything that comes into your head. After you exhale, hold your breath out for a few seconds. During this time between exhaling and inhaling, try to be silent and just listen. Experiment with different arrangements of talking-not talking and inhaling-quiet-exhaling-quiet until you find what works best for you.**

When we are filled with internal talk we cannot pay full attention to what is going on. As one teacher said: "Words get into our ears." We must quiet the internal chatter, let our minds become empty if we are to truly listen and see and touch and smell and taste what is out there. Aldous Huxley put it more strongly: "Words, words, words. They shut one off from the universe. Three quarters of the time one is never in contact with things, only the beastly words which stand for them."

Almost before a sensation enters full awareness, we pigeonhole it with a label and store the label away, neglecting the uniqueness and complexity of the sensation itself. We substitute the label for the reality. We say to ourselves, "Oh, that's a truck going by," and thinking we know all about the sound, the origin of the sound, and its probable destiny, we quit listening. Sometimes this is necessary and useful, for we haven't the time, energy, interest, or brain capacity to pay attention to everything. But when turning off becomes an automatic habit, we become losers. We come more and more to live in the dead world of static and abstract words rather than the live world of things and happenings. We begin to die to reality, victims of language and our language habits.

Our language system, into which we are born without having

any say in the matter, is, of course, vastly important. Although we need it, we are both the beneficiary and the victim of its use and structure. We learn to cut up the universe according to its already prepared categories. Things that don't fit are either ignored or made to fit so that much of their life is squeezed out. We are prejudiced by our language. When we unconsciously identify static words with dynamic processes or mistakenly believe that symbolic abstractions *are* reality we can get into all kinds of trouble—real and psychological. Alfred Korzybski, the founder of general semantics, points out many of these troubles in his text *Science and Sanity*. He also gives some rationale for maintaining internal silence on neurological grounds. The core of his reasoning is based upon the finding that there exists a natural order (in time) of abstracting, proceeding from the external, objective event, to sensations, then to emotions, and lastly to cognitive or associative functions. If a person reverses this natural order by preconceived verbal notions, or blocks it by excessive, continuous internal talking, he reduces his contact with the world. Whereas if he delays or inhibits verbal reactions, he can more fully experience what is going on and react more appropriately.

These exercises in sensory awareness have several aims: to develop your ability to be internally silent when you wish, to expand your consciousness of your sensory world, and to become aware of how you transform that sensory world into words. I will let you discover the other values of these exercises for yourself.

Please note that the most important aim is to achieve control. It *is not* desirable to stop labeling what you hear. It *is not* desirable to stop making inferences about the origins of sensations. It *is* desirable to choose to be silent if you wish. It *is* desirable *to be conscious* of the fact that you are making inferences.

In order to gain control you may find it helpful to observe what happens as you try to listen without verbalizing. How does your mentation process work? What difficulties do you encounter? What per cent successful would you estimate yourself to be? How do you feel after trying the exercises? Writing down your reactions in your notebook after each exercise will help you observe yourself objectively and mark your progress as you proceed.

Just as we are born into a world with its preset language systems, we are born into a culture with its preset values of what is good and bad, what is wrong and right, what is ugly and beautiful. These prejudices lead us to see things in certain ways, and to select some things while excluding others. As we avoid these identifications and prejudices, slipping more into silent, nonverbal awareness, we recover again the perceptual wonderment and richness of childhood. Labeling sounds such as trucks, kids hollering, or doors banging as "noises" is a very common prejudice. Noise annoys us. We become irritable and unpleasant to those around us or generally negative. As a result, we seldom listen to such sounds and in fact exert some effort to actually block them from awareness. In the following exercise, try reversing that process.

Select a sound that you have been categorizing as noise and really listen to it; attempt to maintain internal silence, avoid labeling it or letting your mind wander to other things. Keep focused on the noise. What do you discover?

Try to catch yourself during the day when you label something as a noise. Stop and take a few seconds to listen attentively to it. Our prejudice against "noise" cuts us off from hearing many interesting symphonies of sounds, causing us strain and fatigue.

A more subtle form of prejudice consists of localizing sounds. Because we have ears on each side of our head we learn to relate differences in phase and intensity to differences in location. That a sound originates to my right or left or behind me is an association very like the associations of labels with sounds, and, like the giving of labels, it becomes an automatic process over which we have no control. Try to be aware of sounds altogether without placing them in particular positions outside your body. By inferring the locations of sounds you are actually doing something extra. When you don't localize them, sounds from all around you blend into one harmonious whole.

Neurologically speaking, there are no sounds out there. There exist only patterns of nerve impulses within your brain. When you say that you hear a bird singing in a tree, you have only experienced some electrochemical reactions taking place with your brain, nothing more. Whatever words, thoughts, or inferences you make from that electrochemical reaction pattern are strictly your trip.

As you try to stop the steady stream of nerve impulses we call "internal verbalizing" and be silently, fully, and wholly attentive to your surroundings, you will encounter many difficulties. Your mind will wander to other things; you will feel the need not to waste precious time; you will become frustrated at your inability to control your mind; or you will find a dozen other things more important to do than listen quietly. Do not scold yourself when you fail. Just observe how you function, how you make excuses, or how your mind wanders to other things. Be as detached and as impartial as you can. Try to observe your functioning as if it were someone else's.

Try the same exercises with a different sense:

Take a few minutes each day just to look at things. Let the words cease in your mind for these few minutes—just look without making judgments about what you see, or without responding in any other fashion (save perhaps to walk around objects). If you observe a lot of babbling in your head, let it flow out. Do not try

to command your mind to be quiet. That will only produce strain and tension.

If you try this you will begin to see and enjoy seeing things you never noticed before. Colors and patterns will pop into your awareness and delight you with their simple richness. A row of cars in a parking lot is a symphony of color and pattern if taken as an unmodified sensation. Try attending first to patterns, then only to color. Notice the full three-dimensional aspect of every object. For a real visual feast walk into a department or grocery store and look around. For a thrill that will resonate deep in your nervous system, look at a giant old tree bereft of summer foliage, taking full stock of the patterns the branches make crackling against the sky.

Normally we do not so much look at things as overlook them. Like the ear, the eye sees through a screen of words. We depend on words to organize what the eye sees and to relieve us from the effort of perceiving what is "really there" in specific detail. Once we find the word for things, we "know", and therefore feel secure. For example, some people find abstract art baffling and even disturbing because they can't lean on the crutch of words to help them see. When we erect a screen of verbal symbols the fullness of the world fades. We catch only the rough outlines of things, without color or depth. Take a minute for the following exercise. It will bring back some of the depth of things:

Look at what is around you. Concentrate first on the colors only. How many different colors can you really see? Could you possibly name them all? Next concentrate on the depth of things. How much depth can you perceive? Notice the depth of everything in your visual field.

How much there is to see if we only remember to look. Too few persons ever really see the beauty in the patterns of dirt on a sidewalk, the texture on the bark of a tree, or of an old brick wall. We have become so used to labeling such sights and evaluating them as "dirty," "old," "worthless," etc., that we simply have quit looking at them. They are the analogue of "noises" to the eye.

One of my teachers once told me to "treat every experience as a new experience if you want to be creative." If you try this you will find your sensory life enriched many times over. You will begin to understand what it means not to identify the past with the present and you will seldom be bored by anything.

Touch, one of the most exciting senses, is often the most neglected. We may use the sense of touch to guide our movements during a particular task like typing, writing, eating, throwing a ball, and so on, but we seldom use it for its own sake. Touch is the most vital sense, the most intimate one, the sense which can make us most aware of our own aliveness if we just remember to use it.

Take one minute now to touch whatever is around you. Let your mind become quiet. Hold in abeyance labels, judgments and irrelevant words or thoughts. Feel the texture, the sensory richness of what you are touching. Touch and be touched.

Notice what happens inside your organism when you touch something. What happens in parts of your body that are not touching? What feelings are evoked in you? Do you become relaxed or tense, drowsy or alert after this exercise? Write about your observations and reactions in your notebook. If you have trouble letting your mind become quiet try some of the intermediate exercises for touch like those described for listening. The exercise of coordinating silence with breathing cycles may be especially helpful.

Try touching objects for a minute each day, especially at times when you are tense or tired.

When we talk inside our heads we often contract muscles corresponding to the actions we are talking about. If we worry about actions we will have to perform later we contract muscles that may be antagonistic, and tensions inevitably develop.

When we touch things and try to let the internal chatter cease, two good things happen: we relax, and we come back in contact with the present, with our surroundings. A moment's touching can often permanently interrupt the most vicious and destructive internal cycles of verbalizing. "Keeping in touch" is really very sound advice.

Another neglected sense is taste. We generally acquire many of our tastes and food preferences from our parents and friends. We substitute the prejudices and standards of others for our own and all too often fail to discover, or lose contact with, what we really do like and dislike. The following exercise may help you recover some of this contact.

Try chewing just one bite of food until you have completely pulverized every particle, until it is liquid in your mouth. Keep your attention on your food: when your mind drifts away, bring it back again. Try this with just one bite of food at each meal.

You may quickly find that some foods which you thought ought to taste good actually do not taste good at all, while others have a most exciting taste. Some foods may have a pleasant, superficially good taste but do not sit well in your stomach. Other foods which are bland at first may have an aftertaste of a richness that will astonish you, and that will last and last until the tiniest speck of food is gone from your mouth. As you learn to enhance your taste capacities you may find that your whole being, every cell in your body, welcomes the ingestion of good food. Some people act as if they need a large quantity of food, but may perhaps only be hungry for better-tasting food. They have become greedy for the wrong thing. Try this exercise often and see what you can find out.

Smell, another neglected sense, lends itself readily to the practice of internal silence because we don't have a very complete terminology for smells. We cut out a large fraction of the world of smells because we label so many smells as "stinky" or unpleasant. If you can side-step these acquired prejudices, you may find another part of your world regained.

Although each of us at each moment is capable of sensing nearly everything around us, we frequently live in a state of partial sensory deprivation. Our tragedy is that we don't even realize it. The older we become the more experiences, habits, and learned prejudices take over and direct our sensing, feeling, and thinking. We come to live in a rut that grows deeper with each passing year. Little children are so much more alive to the world than we are. If you can, find some children to guide you back.

Before we can attain extraordinary consciousness we should try to expand our ordinary consciousness to its natural limits. Drugs may temporarily break us out of our cells, but it can be done easily enough without them if we make the initial effort.

The exercises in this chapter are designed to give you a good, strong start. They are also sufficient unto themselves, and if consistently and minutely practiced, they can re-enrich your life.

At first I suggest that you deliberately, consciously try all these exercises once a day. If you set aside a few minutes of total time for them and plan to write in your notebook your thoughts, feelings, and reactions, you will probably benefit the most. It is not easy to change lifelong habit patterns. Only by deliberate *conscious* effort will you achieve much progress. Gradually, your former ways of operating will alter and you will find that you have the control to "tune in" to the rich sensory world around you. The more you bring your daily experience into your consciousness, the more you will really live—and really living here in this world is the secret of getting there.

Perhaps you can begin to understand what the Buddhists mean.

> . . . a world in a grain of sand
> And a heaven in a wild flower.

| III |

Living Here and Now

"What is the way?" asks the disciple.

"Your everyday mind," replies the Master. "When I am hungry, I eat; when tired, I sleep."

The disciple is puzzled, and asks whether this is not what everybody else does too.

"No," the Master replies; "Most people are never wholly in what they are doing; when eating, they may be absent-mindedly preoccupied with a thousand different fantasies; when sleeping, they are not sleeping. The supreme mark of the thoroughly integrated man is to be without a divided mind."

—Zen teaching

"Where are you?" asked my wife across the dinner table in a sorrowful, quizzical tone.

"Oh," I replied, "I was thinking about my book."

"Well, I wish you'd be here with me," she said.

To be totally involved in what you are doing, here and now! It is so easy to write about and so difficult to achieve. We live a good portion of our lives in a state of partial blindness and deafness to our immediate surroundings. We are not nearly as consciously present as we could be, which is not surprising, since

26

no one may ever have told us that we could be, or ought to be, more conscious heretofore. Few people have deemed consciousness-expansion to be a teachable skill worth developing, but without consciousness we function as machines or walking vegetables at best.

How shall we define this mysterious thing called "consciousness"? Let's describe some of its characteristics.

First of all, consciousness varies in degree. When we sleep it is very low, and when we are excited it may be very high, but there exist myriad gradations in between. To what degree are you conscious when you jiggle and bump along on a bus, lost in reveries and daydreams? How active is your consciousness when you brush your teeth? Or drive down the turnpike?

Besides varying in degree, consciousness also varies in breadth. Each sensory channel sends dozens of different inputs to the brain every second. It is impossible to be in full contact with all the things that your senses feed into your brain. You ignore some completely, attend to others partially, and may concentrate on another with complete attention, only to leave it and focus on something entirely different in the next instant.

Consciousness, therefore, weaves a fantastically intricate pattern as it connects you with the world, switching from sensation to sensation and from channel to channel, constantly, all day long—slowing down only when you are sleeping.

Take a minute and jot down in your notebook some things which make you most conscious and some activities which dim your consciousness practically to zero. What turns you off and what turns you on?

Your notes will illustrate an important aspect of consciousness —it is not an abstract isolated state but always involves a relationship between you and the environment. You are not conscious *per se,* you are conscious of something—of a sound, a visual sensation, a touch, a taste, a feeling, or some internal twinge, ache, or tension. Consciousness comprises both the sensations arising from the environment and the self-reflective knowledge of that awareness.

I sense, I know that I sense, therefore I am conscious.

The exercises in Chapter II were designed to help you intensify and expand your sensory awareness, which is one aspect of consciousness. The exercises in this chapter continue that work and bring in a second aspect of consciousness—awareness of yourself in relation to the environment. In addition to improving your ability to live in a more conscious state, these exercises will give you energy. Their basic aim is to develop your ability to be present and fully engaged in whatever you are doing.

Write down what you are immediately aware of. Write down all the sensations that enter your consciousness as rapidly as you can. Try not to deviate from the present time. Include every area of sensation that you can, both internal and external, feelings as well as movements. Work for about one minute.

For example, your sentences might read like this: "Now I'm aware of a car going by. Now I'm aware of my legs being crossed. Now I'm aware of writing, of my pencil scratching on the paper, of the wind noises. Now I'm aware of feeling frustrated, of blinking, of tensions in my shoulders. Now I'm aware that I stopped writing and was daydreaming, of wanting to stop this, of rubbing my elbows on the desk."

Try the exercise now if you haven't yet done so.

What happened? Did you find it possible to capture every conscious sensation in writing? At what point were you overwhelmed with the task of trying to observe them all with any completeness? What per cent of their total would you estimate that you wrote down? Look your list over to see if you have omitted any areas of potential awareness. Did you note smells? Did you note things like the pressure of the chair against your buttocks and back? Were you frustrated by the notion of immediate awareness? You probably observed that as soon as you began to write about what you were aware of, the experience had passed and you were aware of something else. Hence, you might have concluded that the exercise is virtually impossible and stopped doing it.

This paradoxical time lag between experience and awareness often puzzles people, making it difficult for them to undertake the exercises. Here is an explanation which may be helpful:

Just as awareness spans some finite sensory dimension such as a small range of tones, colors, smells, etc., it also spans some finite interval of time. Experiments show that a minimum interval of time for detailed perception lasts about one tenth of a second for most senses. Hence your "now" spans at least that interval of ordinary duration. It may range from that lower limit to an hour or more but will usually be in the neighborhood of a few tenths of a second.

The diagram in Figure 2, looking like a normal distribution curve from statistics, may help you understand the use of "now." Time is represented on the horizontal axis and the vertical axis represents the magnitude of attention focused by the power of consciousness on some thing or event. The mean, or center of the curve, represents "now" or the present instant.

At any given instant one's attention is primarily concentrated in the present moment but contains awareness of events from the past and awareness of anticipated events of the future.

Generally, we do not have as clear a perception of the immediate future as we do of the recent past—so a more representative curve would not be symmetrical about the present, but would show a sharp drop on the right. Figure 3 illustrates this situation.

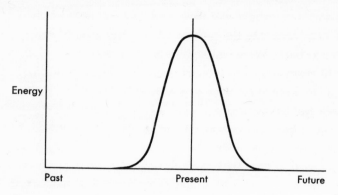

Figure 3. Typical time distribution of "now."

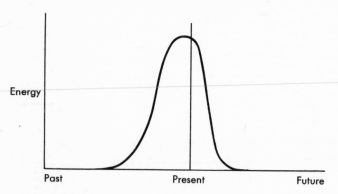

Figure 2. Symmetrical time distribution of "now."

The attention curve might be drawn high and narrow to represent an intense focus with little cognition of the past and anticipated future, or it might be drawn broad and low to represent an extended awareness of some ongoing experience. For example, I may be keenly aware of the swirl of a butterfly across my vision. The event may last only a couple of seconds; the before and the anticipated future are insignificant. The curve would be narrow and steep. Or, in listening to a symphony I may be intensely absorbed in what is happening in the present, but I am also conscious of what has gone before in the symphony and mentally alert to an anticipated development of the theme as well. A diagram describing this would extend more into the past and into the future.

I will develop this model in more detail in Chapter IV, but let's return to the task of developing your power to live more consciously. Try the basic exercise again, but do not write this time.

Say aloud, or silently, what you are immediately aware of right now. Begin each sentence or phrase with: "Now I'm aware of . . ." Be as complete as possible.

Perhaps from this second attempt you learned more about the operation of consciousness. Could you be aware of the time span of your consciousness as you switched from one stimulus to another? Did you keep going strongly or were there pauses in your verbalizing? If you stopped momentarily, why did you do so? Did some stimulus trigger you into daydreams, reveries, or cause you to drift off into thinking about the future while temporarily losing contact with immediate sensations? If you did something like this, were you aware of doing it? Or were you only afterward aware that you had been doing it? If so, what then brought you back to continuing the exercise?

Your first attempts at this exercise will probably show you how easily and unconsciously your attention flits from sensation to sensation, and then slips easily into free and aimless wanderings in the dim alleyways of your mind, which are of about as much value as the random reading of old newspapers.

Consciousness is a slippery thing: as soon as we think to ask if we are conscious, our attention turns elsewhere by itself; consciousness, the director of attention, usually slips away, only to reappear, sparked into existence by seemingly trivial events or governed by laws beyond our ken. When I am fully conscious, however, my experience is qualitatively different. It seems as if the impressions arising from my environment go to a different place within me—a place where I can use them better or get more from them.

Our organisms continually abstract from the environment, filtering, and codifying thousands of lights, sounds, smells, tastes, and pressures into images and symbols. Work with hypnosis and direct electrical stimulation of the brain has shown that much, if not all, of this material registers in the incredibly precise and enormously large memory of the brain, although it may be ordinarily beyond our ability to recall. To the extent that we can register more of our experiencing by *consciously* directing our attention to it we enrich and expand our lives—for our *real* life consists of our conscious moments.

The basic exercise in the practice of being present in the moment will help you repossess severed nonverbal realms of experience. Don't expect to be able to do this for more than a few seconds at the start, but keep trying, verbalizing "Now I am aware . . ." until you get the feeling that "Now" and "I" and the object of awareness constitute a unified whole.

Here is a deceptively simple little exercise that will give you a measure of your progress.

Look at the second hand of a watch or clock for one minute. Focus all the attention you can on the tip of the second hand. Let your mind be still. Do not verbalize internally about anything. Just look, but do not strain or stare.

Exercises in developing consciousness are frustratingly difficult —that is why they are called exercises. Be tolerant toward your behavior; regard the exercises as games you play with yourself.

The above exercise is valuable because you will have a direct and immediate measure of your progress. You will know what per cent of the time you are successful, and how many seconds your consciousness sleeps during each minute. Try to observe your mentation process. See what makes consciousness enter and leave. What can you discover about the rules of "The Master Game"?

A very good time to try playing the game of here and now is when you are out walking:

Try to be fully here and now as you walk along. To get started verbalize to yourself at first: "Now I'm aware of the sound of my feet on the ground. Now I'm aware of looking at the person walking toward me. Now I'm aware of the sun shining on my face." And so on. Let the words die away but keep your attention on as much of what is happening as possible.

Did you find after a few seconds that you were lost in thoughts very far from the here and now and then suddenly came to when an unusually strong stimulus penetrated your fog of verbalizing? Trace your thought patterns back and try to recall what made your consciousness depart. This may give you some useful clues about how your mechanical mind works and how powerful it is. You may find it helpful to keep a written record of what causes you to leave the here and now.

At first, simply trying to be here and now while walking may be too big a task. Try selecting only a short interval, say the time from stepping off a curb to stepping onto the one across the street. Or decide that you will try to be conscious only while walking from one particular tree to the end of the block. After you have made such an effort, relax, and let your mind pursue its own course. Don't strain, just make a game of it.

Try the exercises whenever you have the opportunity, but, if you can, schedule at least a few minutes each day for several real efforts and jot down your observations and reactions in your notebook.

At first you will probably find it helpful to verbalize by the formula: "Now I'm aware of . . ." After a while try to be conscious without verbalizing. See if you can reach a state of knowing without thinking. "Thought is the expression of experience, it is not experiencing," Jiddu Krishnamurti wrote. "Thought is a response of memory. As long as there is thinking there can be no experiencing." When you think: "I'm seeing a flower" the experience is already in the past. Thinking quickly blots out experiencing and takes you away from the present.

I have found that attending to my breathing is one of the best ways to quiet thought and unify the experiencing of the world with the feeling of myself. If I coordinate my breathing with the two aspects of consciousness described earlier—sensing the world and knowing that I am sensing it—then being here and now becomes much easier.

As you breathe in, pay attention to the sensations arising from your environment, draw them into you. As you breathe out, be aware of "you" as being present in those sensations. There is no need to take deep breaths or control your breathing in any way; simply let your attention alternate from the world to yourself as you inhale and exhale. Breathe in air and take in the world. Breathe out air and be aware of yourself, simply, easily, quietly, without strain or effort.

As an experiment reverse the breathing, how does this feel to you?

This exercise connects a physiological process with a psychological one. The integration should feel natural and effortless. While doing it, I make no forcible attempt to control either my breathing or my mind. I merely focus my attention first on my impressions, and then on remembering myself. The two parts of the exercise make up a complete unit of consciousness. The exercise also uses a natural unit of time, that of one's breathing cycle, to define the here and now.

This is a key exercise. Integrate it with other exercises in this and succeeding chapters. You can always make the effort to coordinate breathing with the two aspects of consciousness—awareness of the environment, and awareness of yourself as present in the environment in the midst of practically any activity. Even the most feeble efforts, if consistently followed through, will result in permanent and beneficial changes. For instance, consider the whole area of movement and internal sensations. As we walk, sit, or move about we constantly tense and relax the muscles in our bodies. Often we tense whole sets of muscles unnecessarily and leave them partially tense for hours, days, or sometimes years. Such chronic tensions are analogous to needless thoughts, and like daydreams, fantasies, and worries they result in tragic wastes of energy. No wonder so many people tire easily, become depressed, or feel chronically low in energy. Careful and consistent efforts to be aware of internal sensations and tensions will help you eliminate many of these internal patterns of behavior.

To expand your consciousness of your physical organism try the following exercise:

Lie down, but do not deliberately relax. Be aware of sensations arising from the external world for a few minutes, then concentrate on internal sensations arising from your organism. Get the feel of your body as a whole, forming an image in your mind of how your body looks. Let your attention glide systematically through every part of your body. Then coordinate your breathing with this. As you inhale, be aware of the internal sensations from your organism. As you exhale let yourself flow into your body. Let your attention wander systematically through your legs, lower trunk, chest, arms, neck, and head. If you find your body lying crookedly, gently readjust your position. Especially attend to those parts of your organism which ordinarily you dislike because they are inadequate in some respect—such as

eyes, stomach, teeth, skin, and so on. Try to hold in abeyance such negative evaluations—just observe as impartially and as fully as you can.

Many debilitating illnesses arise simply because we unconsciously let our physical organisms get out of balance. We forget to pay attention to our bodies, treating them like slaves, driving them unmercifully until they finally rebel. A little kindness would be in order, a little understanding, a little conscious consideration.

Often, we waste a lot of energy fuming about some chore that we must do but don't want to do, such as going to the store, painting the house, washing the floor, or cleaning out the basement. In such a case try this, one of the very best here-and-now experiments:

Choose a chore that you have to do frequently, such as washing dishes, sweeping the floor, brushing your teeth, or carrying out the garbage, and try to be fully here and now with that task as you carry it out. If you drift away, catch yourself and come back. Enter fully into doing that task. Notice as much as you possibly can. Expand your sensory awareness to the maximum. Don't evaluate any of your sensations in terms of likes and dislikes, good and bad, beautiful and ugly; just experience them. Write down your reactions, thoughts, and feelings.

If you really give this a try, not just think about it as you read these words, I predict the results will delight you. And you will be on your way to your:

EVERY-MINUTE ZEN

Zen students are with their masters at least ten years before they presume to teach others. Nan-in was visited by Tenno, who, having passed his apprenticeship, had become a teacher. The day happened to be rainy, so Tenno wore wooden clogs and carried an umbrella. After greeting him, Nan-in remarked:

"I suppose you left your wooden clogs in the vestibule. I want to know if your umbrella is on the right or the left side of the clogs." Tenno, confused, had no instant answer. He realized that he was unable to carry his Zen every minute. He became Nan-in's pupil, and he studied six more years to accomplish his every-minute Zen.

—*Zen Flesh, Zen Bones*

| IV |

Transcending Here and Now

Alice carefully released the brush, and did her best to get the Queen's hair into order. "Come, you look rather better now!" she said, after altering most of the pins. "But really you should have a lady's-maid!"

"I'm sure I'll take *you* with pleasure!" the Queen said. "Twopence a week, and jam every other day."

Alice couldn't help laughing, as she said "I don't want you to hire *me*——and I don't care for jam."

"It's very good jam," said the Queen.

"Well, I don't want any *to-day,* at any rate."

"You couldn't have it if you *did* want it," the Queen said. "The rule is, jam to-morrow and jam yesterday——but never jam *to-day.*"

"It *must* come sometimes to 'jam to-day,'" Alice objected.

"No, it can't" said the Queen. "It's jam every *other* day: to-day isn't any *other* day, you know."

"I don't understand you," said Alice. "It's dreadfully confusing!"

—Lewis Carroll

You probably know people who are so busy reliving past events that they never seem to enjoy the present, and frequently do their best to spoil it for others.

"Last time we were here we had lobster with sweet sauce. It was simply marvelous, and poor Janie spilled hers in her lap, and we all laughed and laughed, and . . . blah blah blah . . ."

Other people seem always to be in such a hurry to get to tomorrow, that magical place and time when everything will be good and beautiful, that they sacrifice today. They'll sacrifice you, too, if you let them.

"I can't possibly go today, got to work, but tomorrow—if I get this work done—I will surely go with you and then the sun will be out and we will have fun. Why don't you stay home and go with me tomorrow?"

But when tomorrow comes, these self-appointed martyrs won't be there, you can be sure. They will be hard at work planning for the day after next.

Although it is often necessary to work, the question is: Where is your consciousness focused? If focused on tomorrow or yesterday then you lose today no matter what you do.

Not only do we get sidetracked by the past or the future, but as if that weren't enough, we also often spin off into fantasy worlds that couldn't possibly happen.

"Now if I had said "YES" to George yesterday, then we would have gone to Pyramid Peak and surely found that mercury mine, and . . . blah blah blah . . ."

How often do you go off on "if trips," imagining that you inherited a million dollars or suddenly developed the power to breathe under water, be a champion tennis player, or joined James Bond in some racy adventure?

Our language permits us to think in imaginary space-time. The fact that we have the subjunctive mode, the "might have been" form of expression, permits us to verbalize about conditions that never did or never could occur. This mode is valuable for certain purposes, such as planning an activity and taking into account possible contingencies, but it can lead us to fritter away our hours in all sorts of nonsense. We can, for instance, experience *real* feelings of guilt or suffering from purely *imaginary* events. These feelings can produce muscle tensions, hormone changes, and all types of effects on our organisms as well as on the people around us. Tension and anxiety often result from imagined future unpleasantness. Sometimes we correctly perceive the course of future events and our anxiety motivates us to act appropriately, but when we become tense and anxious over past events or events from the world of "if," then we are really being silly.

"I should have done such and such—Oh dear, what a fool I was. If only I had . . ." We do much of our living in imaginary space-time, and, unfortunately, do it automatically and unconsciously. Continual if-tripping leads nowhere; it only saps our energies, weakens our will even further, and leaves us with no real freedom. It is always "jam tomorrow" and "jam yesterday"—but never jam today.

One reason it is difficult for us to be in full contact with our experiencing is because we have so often been forced to do things we don't want to do. We've been carefully taught all kinds of likes and dislikes, and we've learned all sorts of escape and avoidance techniques. We are so accustomed to being bored or frustrated in school from the age of six on, to being yelled at or cruelly punished for childish sins, or to being molded into machines by our technocratic society, that we have all concocted expert disappearing acts. We can leave the scene at a millisecond's notice. When things get rough we slip off to our fantasy worlds and safely wait out the storm. Some of us stay there, locked in for a lifetime. Mostly we come and go, but not of our own free will. We are driven by the will of others or, more likely, by the random accidental circumstances of our day, coupled with numberless preconceived ideas of what is good and bad, pleasant and unpleasant, acceptable or taboo, and true or false.

As an exercise:

Write down three statements beginning with: "I should . . ."

How do these statements keep you from the here and now? Do your statements really come from your inner needs or are they other people's trips that have been laid on you? Are they lies that have been unthinkingly accepted by you?

When others lie to us, they are trying to warp our view of reality; when we lie to ourselves, we split into fragments. Instead of accepting what is, we partition from reality what we wish to be. One part of us sustains the wish, while another part admits the full truth. The part that knows the truth must either pretend that it does not know, or go into hiding in the deeper chambers of our minds. When we are so fragmented, how can we live in the present?

Here is a difficult exercise for you:

Write down three lies that you tell yourself. How many pieces of you can you identify which have arisen from these three lies?

For example, I tell myself that I am an honest man. But part of me knows full well all the times I've been dishonest. The first part goes parading around saying, "I'm an honest man," but the second part always whispers off stage of my dishonest actions. Sometimes the two parts fight and sometimes they make a truce for a while. When they fight, a great deal of energy may be wasted.

I tell myself that I love my wife, denying the fact that sometimes I hate her. I never tell her this. One part loves her, one part hates her, a third part denies the existence of the hating part. How can I be so many different i's? If I shrink from bringing into full consciousness any unpleasantness, I can only be partly here and now with my surroundings. Perform the experiment yourself.

If you suffer a physical or psychological hurt, try letting it come fully into your conscious awareness. Don't run away from it. Focus on what is actually happening within your organism. Then, if you choose to leave the present, do so consciously, by deliberate action rather than mechanical reaction. You can develop the power to be master of your attention.

In general, whenever you try one of these experiments and wake up realizing that you have been asleep and far away from the present, go back and ask what possible fear, lie, or unresolved need triggered your departure.

It is hard to live in the present. We are always being pursued by the twin beasts of the past and the future which nibble away at our energy and our time. A Zen parable makes the point.

> A man traveling across the field encountered a tiger. He fled, the tiger after him. Coming to a precipice, he caught hold of the root of a wild vine and swung himself down over the edge. The tiger sniffed at him from above. Trembling, the man looked down to where, far below, another tiger was waiting to eat him. Only the vine sustained him. Two mice, one white and one black, little by little started to gnaw away the vine. The man saw a luscious strawberry near him. Grasping the vine with one hand, he plucked the strawberry with the other. How sweet it tasted.
>
> —*Zen Flesh, Zen Bones*

How often the fruits of the present escape our notice.

If you watch yourself impartially you will soon see how your attention wanders almost at random through real and imaginary universes. Each little stimulus triggers a preprogramed set of associations and starts chains of thought which, in turn, lead to others, taking you to and fro across the here and now, if-tripping into other worlds and back again. As soon as you think you are here—you are not.

At first you will be helpless to do anything about your

automatic record playing, you probably won't even observe it clearly; you will be caught up in the streams of internal conversations. After a while, though, you will become more alert to the internal babbling of your mentation process and be better able to control your attention.

Do not scold yourself if you cannot continuously focus on the present. In fact, it is not always necessary or desirable. To let our minds play with fantasies, alternative events, or just idly free-associate constitutes the chief source of our creativity. It can also be tremendously relaxing. Sometimes you may want to escape from a difficult or unpleasant situation by turning your mind to other things. But remember that you have a choice. Sometime when you are bored or idle, try deliberately leaving the here-now and going to a very pleasant place or event from your past or into an imaginary one. Make a slight effort to ignore your present surroundings and stay in that pleasant place for a few moments. Then deliberately return your attention to the present. You will probably find yourself refreshed and able to continue with renewed energy to the task at hand.

Sometimes you may find it hard to stay in the here and now because some unfinished situation needs taking care of by action or thought. In such a case go there deliberately, willfully, and attend to your business.

Then deliberately, willfully return to the here and now. Relax and let your mind wander where ever it chooses. Try to keep a part of your consciousness observing the wanderings of the rest. Write down your reactions, thoughts, or feelings as well as particular places or situations which you wander to. If you come upon any unfinished situations or problems, write down what you need to do to finish them. Follow this with an attempt to be fully present to your immediate surroundings.

Living in the past, or the anticipated future, or some world of "if" usually wastes energy. Remembering and anticipating are valid and useful activities but a difference exists between actively and consciously remembering an event and mechanically reliving it. There is a difference between active planning for the future by consciously considering alternatives, and idly living in daydreams. Living *fully* in the present includes taking note of past experience or future probabilities and modifying one's present behavior on the basis of that knowledge. One measure of intelligence involves how much a man takes into account, in his present behavior, the past and future. The simple here-now awareness of a puppy is not the here-now consciousness of which a human being is capable.

We dwell at length on our hurts and sorrows, perhaps more than on our pleasures, but neither does much good. To help you clarify such situations try the following exercises:

1. **Write the names of three situations or persons which resulted in great hurts, tragedies, or difficulties for you.**
2. **Now index those situations or persons as to time and place. Write down the place and the time or time period of the hurt. Be as specific as possible.**
3. **Turn to the end of this chapter (p. 54) for the third step in this exercise.**

Many of us find it hard to be in the present because we carry around too much of the past. We adhere to past situations and this attachment keeps us from being in the here and now.

MUDDY ROAD

Tanzan and Ekido were once traveling together down a muddy road. A heavy rain was still falling. Coming around a bend, they met a lovely girl in a silk kimono and sash, unable to cross the intersection.

"Come on, girl," said Tanzan at once. Lifting her in his arms, he carried her over the mud.

Ekido did not speak again until that night when they reached a lodging temple. Then he could no longer restrain himself.

"We monks don't go near females," he told Tanzan, "especially not young and lovely ones. It is dangerous. Why did you do that?"

"I left the girl there," said Tanzan, "Are you still carrying her?"

—*Zen Flesh, Zen Bones*

Pleasurable past events can attach us as strongly as unpleasurable ones. How often have you felt the melancholy sweet pain of past pleasures? We may get away with this now and then, but we cannot continually substitute remembered or imaginary living for real living any more than we can live by watching TV. The energy that goes into imagination or remembrance detracts from the energy available for being here in the present, and may slowly turn us into mechanical zombies.

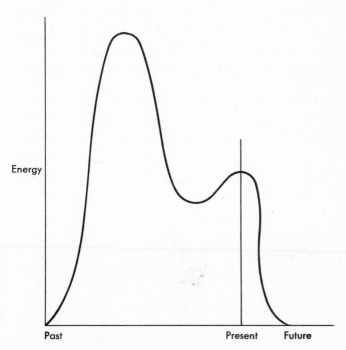

Figure 4. A hang-up of psychological energy.

We all know people who seem to have little of the spark of life. They walk around as if in a trance, or seem apathetic and joyless. This is not an either/or situation, of course, and happens to each of us in varying degrees. If we strongly cling to past events, and are not free to attend to the present, our energy flow is blocked. Figure 4, which illustrates this situation, may be considered as a visual representation of a "hang-up." Energy focused or concentrated upon something in the past, literally gets "hung up" there. It may, of course, be focused on some future event rather than a past one, or on some event that could never happen (in which case, I suppose, it would be appropriate to introduce imaginary coordinates for representing this in the diagram).

Our attention is actually multidimensional, not one dimensional like this enormously simplified diagram. We have thousands of big and little hang-ups which fight for our energy every second. A more realistic diagram might look like this:

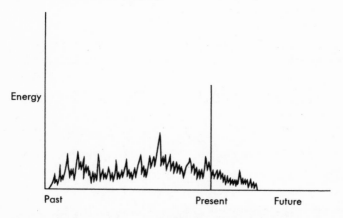

Figure 5. Typical energy distribution among many hang-ups.

By making efforts to focus on the here and now we can begin to drain off energy from all those little hang-ups. However, there is a paradox here: if hang-ups keep us from being here and now, how can we be here-now and drain energy from the hang-ups? The resolution of the paradox is simple. If we make an effort to be present, however feeble and sporadic, then we are putting a little less energy into past hang-ups or imaginary living. If we attend to our environment, then we begin to *gain energy* instead of losing it. The process is circular and positive, for if we live consciously, more in the present, more in the here-now we can more easily prevent the waste of energy elsewhere. Living consciously in the present is a way of side-stepping most of one's minor hang-ups. It is a bootstrap operation which involves neither psychoanalytic reconstruction of particular incidents nor painful private introspection. It is not, however, either magical or easy.

Living in the here and now requires hard, persistent work, starting with daily practice on small matters, so that one can be prepared and strengthened for big crises. I remember a time a few years ago when I was under tremendous psychological strain. I was trying with all my might just to concentrate on eating a cookie. I couldn't do it. Worries and anxieties kept swarming into my head, overwhelming me with despair. But I kept trying, and because I had practiced for years when there were no great strains on me, I did succeed at last. Day after day, at that time of my life, I hung on to little bits of the here and now and kept myself anchored, managing to avoid being swept away into depression and illness.

Practice with these exercises is not by itself the best or quickest road to physical and mental health and higher consciousness. Friends and professional therapists, teachers, or gurus—all can help.

A person is not solely responsible for his hang-ups or the diversion of his life's energies away from the present. But if he makes the choice to free his energies and asks for help and works on his own, he will make progress. Parents, teachers, peers, cultural and linguistic traditions, customs, mores, and habits, all contribute to form a person's character and determine how he directs his energy. Moreover, the process of living generates blocks and hang-ups of various sorts. No one can do exactly as he pleases as long as there are other people in the world. Some frustration is bound to occur, and intense or prolonged frustration can permanently tie up energy in desires for revenge, self-pity, or if-tripping. A good therapist or a considerate friend can help us free ourselves from self-destructive patterns of behavior.

Also, nearly everyone suffers a few major and minor accidents as he grows up. In working with people as a therapist I have observed that pain or severe fright sometimes literally scared a person's consciousness temporarily out of his brain and body. Car accidents, skiing accidents, falling from high places, surgical operations, etc., all may produce this effect.

Pain and fright reactions may be permanently imprinted on the body as muscular contractions, spasms, tensions, or blocks to the expression of feeling and free action. These blocks tie up a person's energies, reducing the amount available for use in the present—for contacting the world and communicating with other people. In the process of treatment I try to get the person to relive the traumatic situation, with his consciousness fully engaged, re-experiencing the pain, fear, tension, etc., and thus reconnecting to his body. Then the body relaxes and energy flows more freely.

A person can release some of his blocks on his own by practicing the exercises, by understanding what is going on, and by trying to stay with the present situation, no matter how unpleasant or painful. In severe situations, however, a therapist is essential, particularly in untying knots from the past.

Consciousness cannot be drawn as a continuous smooth curve,

but as a highly variable one, with many ups and downs. Big accidents and painful stressors drive us away from contact or eliminate consciousness altogether. To a smaller extent, little unpleasantnesses during the course of each day also diminish consciousness. One of the best exercises to help you develop a more continuous consciousness is to "unroll the day" each night before sleeping.

Before retiring sit or lie quietly and try to visualize your entire day from the moment of arising to the present. Do not verbalize. Try to let the day's events unroll like a movie film. If your mind wanders, start over. If there are gaps in your memory, go on as best as you can.

This is a difficult exercise, but a valuable one. When you try it, you will quickly find out how much of the day you spend in unconscious sleep. By making the effort to recall your day, you will find it easier to be present on the succeeding day. Then that day will be recalled with greater clarity. Try the exercise for a few days, then let it go for a while, and return to it at a later date.

As you gradually increase your ability to be here-now with your environment and with your own person you might feel ready to try it with other people. Truly being present with another person is one of the finest possible experiences. To begin with:

Be here-now with someone for a few minutes of conversation. Stay in the present when you talk even if the other does not. Afterward write your thoughts, feelings, and reactions in your notebook.

Here's one comment from a student's notebook:

When I did this exercise I began to realize the full significance of being (or *not* being) here and now with another person. If I do not stay in the here and now it means very little that another person is there. If the other person is not here and now, I get the feeling that I am not a person at all but merely a thing—an object which happens incidentally to be occupying a particular space. If neither of us is here and now it seems rather unimportant from the standpoint of a relationship that we are in physical proximity at all.

Can you think of ways to stop another person from leaving the here and now? Or do you know how you can bring a person back after he has left?

If you have a friend who has been introduced to these notions you might like to try the following exercise with him or her:

> **Sit in a quiet place where you can easily see and hear and touch the other. Try to stay in the immediate here and now when you talk. When past events or future plans are being discussed, bring them actively into the now as you communicate.**
>
> **Coordinate your breathing patterns with each other. As you breathe in, take in the other and his communication. As you breathe out give youself to the other. Gradually let talking cease but continue communicating.**

Real communication is a joyful experience.

After you have experienced this with one friend, acquaint a few others with the experience and try a group experiment.

> **In a group of not more than five persons, sit close together, so that each person can see everyone else. Begin by shutting your eyes and taking in internal sensations of your body. Go over all the parts of the body in systematic fashion, relaxing any tensions. Then everyone should open their eyes and verbalize what they are immediately aware of, out loud, all at once. After a minute of this, try to be fully present with each other in conversation. Ignore other aspects in the room, your own internal sensations, or any other external sensations not directly connected with others in the group. In addition, each group member must assume the responsibility of alerting others who appear to have lost contact with the group, by gently touching them or speaking to them: saying perhaps "Where are you?" or something**

appropriate. After a while, let talking cease, but stay with each other. Maintain eye contact.

Do not attempt to work too long in a group—ten minutes is enough. It will probably tire you at first, and also produce some strong feelings. As one person in one group said: "I felt like I just had to scream with joy," and, when everyone else echoed his statement, he did.

There is another way of working in a group that you might like to try:

In a group of not more than five persons sit close together so that everyone can see and touch everyone else. Repeat the first portion of the previous exercise. Then let members of the group focus their attention on one individual and make an effort to bring that person intensely into the present. Everyone looks at the person and that person simply looks back at each member in turn or as he chooses. The group members may coordinate their breathing if they wish, but it is not necessary. They may talk, although it is sometimes difficult. About a minute's attention for each person is usually sufficient.

To be consciously here-now is a most difficult thing—but rewarding. To achieve it in a group is more difficult and even more rewarding. Having everyone else help you, pulling you into a super state of here-now, is an ecstatic experience.

If you are seriously trying these exercises and make some efforts to continue them you may have some strange experiences. These will not be harmful or frightening, in fact they will probably be accompanied by feelings of joyfulness, elation, timelessness, or ineffable beauty. For brief seconds or minutes, perhaps longer, these feelings may persist, then gradually fade away. You will have passed from what I call the "simple here-now" to a glimpse of the "transcendental here-now." You will have touched a higher consciousness, not ordinarily present in our daily living.

The difference between these states can be crudely represented by the following diagrams:

Figure 5 represents our usual state, with energy dissipated elsewhere than the present and consciousness at a low level. As a man begins to make efforts, collects his consciousness, and focuses his attention on the present, he comes, at least momentarily, into a state of being simply here-now (Figure 6).

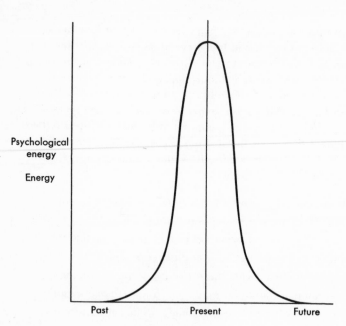

Figure 6. Focused on the simple here-now.

If he makes further efforts and gains more energy the curve would heighten and broaden (Figure 7), taking into account more of the past and more of the future. Ultimately the curve might heighten and broaden indefinitely and at the limit it would become a high, practically flat line. This represents a transcendental state, where all of time is apprehended now.

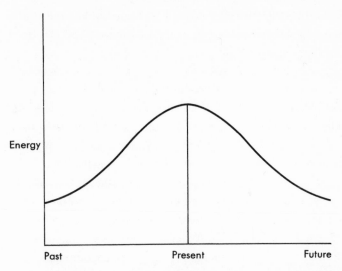

Figure 7. Expansion of simple here-now into the transcendental here-now.

The transcendental state may also be generated from the simple here-now state by another process.* If you consider that the curve in Figure 6 represents only one unit of the present (perhaps the duration of a conscious breath), you can imagine a succession of such curves moving along the time line as the present moves. This movement would sweep out and generate a broad curve ultimately approaching the transcendental state. Such an integration only occurs if, or to the extent that, a man is actively present. Then, the impressions which he absorbs remain with him in succeeding instants and enter into his future

*Don't let your thinking become fixated on these diagrams, which are merely my own simplistic models. The diagrams may be useful for the intellect but they do not necessarily match the reality of your experience.

experiencing instead of just fading away as they do with most of us most of the time. This is rather like the difference between watching a movie and fully living. The former is passive; it comes and goes across our present, leaving little trace on the course of our lives, whereas our conscious living accumulates and can build toward a transcendental state.

Sometimes you may obtain a flash of higher consciousness by being intensely here-now with some ordinary or extraordinary event, or perhaps a moment of communion with a loved one. At such times energy is drained from all your big and little hang-ups and made available for the moment. You may experience a sense of great peace and tranquillity and a feeling of togetherness within yourself and with the universe. These flashes occur only temporarily, especially at first. The energy curve would be drawn as very high, but probably not very broad. As you make efforts, the flashes may become more frequent and of longer duration, until the transcendental moments of your living become its entirety.

Exercise: Step 3.
Then ask yourself the following questions. How much of each situation is still present with me even as I read this book? Or as I go about my business of the day? What is the relationship *now*, this moment, of the people who once were troublesome to me? How much energy am I diverting to those situations or persons right now?

An instant realization sees endless time.
Endless time is as one moment.
When one comprehends the endless moment
He realizes the person who is seeing it.

—Zen teaching

| V |

Meditation

Meditation can be learned, and it must be practiced
according to accepted rules. By its means it is possible to
realize the personal Brahman, who, in union with Maya,
creates, preserves, and dissolves the universe, and likewise
the impersonal Brahman, who transcends all forms of being,
who eternally is, without attributes and without action.

—*The Upanishads*

Meditation is one of the classical ways of "getting there without
drugs." Like the notion of here-now, it seems trivially obvious,
but its simplicity is deceptive. The purposes of meditation are: (1)
to produce perfect alignment of the emotions, the physical body,
and the mentation process; (2) to contact a higher self or
consciousness which transcends the ordinary personality of the
physical organism; and (3) to bring that higher consciousness into
operation in your daily life through your physical body.

In Chapter IV, I suggested that a similar higher consciousness
or "self" could be touched whenever one is truly and fully
here-now with all the elements of his environment (both external
and internal). In one sense, meditation is a natural outgrowth of
being here-now, for on its most elementary level it is merely an

awareness of one's mentation process. Meditation is not an escape from life into a mental hermitage, but rather a positive, dynamic process producing vitality and self-renewal for the ordinary needs of living in this world. In its basic form, meditation constitutes a kind of mental truce, a period for regaining serenity and composure. While sleep gives rest to the brain, nervous system, and body, it may not rest the mind. Meditation rests the mind. The practice of meditation can be very worthwhile for this purpose alone, with no concern about contacting your higher consciousness or achieving a mystical state.

There are many teachers of meditation and many books on the subject—you can investigate where you please but try to avoid the trap of substituting reading for doing. The techniques set forth here are ones that I have personally found useful.

To begin meditation, assume any comfortable position that can be maintained for about fifteen minutes. It is not necessary to sit in the familiar lotus position with crossed and folded legs. You may wish to start lying down—if you can do so without falling asleep. Or, perhaps, you have a favorite old stuffed chair which you sit in by the hour. If you have sufficient muscle tone, you may be able to sit erect on a chair without using the back, or on a cushion on the floor. Whatever position you find comfortable will be the best one—at least in the beginning. Experiment with positions later if you wish. The chief aim is to place your body in such a position that no physical strains are created and only minimum attention need be given to your physical self.

After you have settled yourself, close your eyes and try to relax all the muscles of your body. Begin by relaxing the muscles around the eyes. Check to see if the eyeballs are resting against the back of the eye sockets. Let your attention move slowly around the ring of muscles which circle your eye, first one eye

and then the other. Attend to the scalp muscles, the cheeks, and muscles around the mouth. Proceed down the back of the neck around the shoulders, down the back, out one arm into each of your fingers separately, one by one. Return again up your arm and across your chest, then down into your other arm and hand as before. Then proceed to focus your attention progressively into your stomach, pelvis, hips, legs, and feet. The more detailed and discriminatory your attention, the more you will benefit.

After you have done this warm-up activity, attend to your process of mentation. Don't try to think of anything in particular or to stop thinking completely. Simply observe how thoughts arise, what kind of automatic associations triggers them, and how they in turn trigger different thoughts. Can you observe without being caught up and carried along in the stream? This is the aim, this is the first goal of meditation.

Meditation should be practiced regularly for at least thirty days to give you any kind of satisfying results. For best results I recommend that you:

1. **Do it morning and evening.**
2. **Sit in the same place.**
3. **Sit in the same position.**
4. **Face in the same direction.**
5. **Try it for no more than fifteen minutes at a sitting.**

Although similar to the exercises in Chapters III and IV on being here and now, meditation is much harder. The second hand of a watch or the feel of a tree trunk are pretty objective and unchanging things compared to the thoughts in one's head. Thoughts come and go, mix and blend, like notes and themes in a symphony, carrying your attention away in the development of a fugue, rondo, or in the recapitulation.

If you watch your mentation process closely, you will realize that you don't think thoughts—they just happen. *It* thinks. We can choose the topic we want to "think" about, but the thoughts themselves just come to us. We do not have control over them, we more or less have to wait for them and we can do little to hasten the process.

Try different experiments as you meditate. For instance, if you realize that you are daydreaming or having a weird fantasy, don't stop it; let the daydream unfold, but watch it with consciousness apart. Then after the daydream is finished, trace back your thoughts until you reach the stimulus which triggered that daydream. Be curious and impartial. Pretend that you are tuned into someone else's mind, and that you can't predict what will be verbalized or visualized.

Perhaps you will be interested in these comments from a student's paper:

> If you think meditation is sissy stuff, strictly for fat pseudo-buddhas or semi-gurus, just try it buddy! It makes mountain climbing, country-road jogging, or skin diving seem pretty tame. I have never struggled so fiercely at anything as trying to keep conscious and impartial during meditation period. And the very act of struggling is itself a wrongness which must be struggled against. I seem constantly to be against myself for being against myself. As soon as I think I am succeeding I am lost. Whenever I think myself winning, then I am losing. Every tiny success carries the shadow of defeat, for to evaluate something as success is to fail to be impartial, to be caught up with the thing itself rather than standing apart from it. I start over, carefully, laboriously, knowing that at any instant all will be lost. My fifteen minutes seems like an eternity and it is with a sigh of relief that I return to my sleep, to my ordinary existence. But I know that the peak is there to be scaled and my sleep is never so sound as in the old days.

Thoreau was right when he wrote: ". . . it is easier to sail many thousands of miles through cold and storm and cannibals, in a government ship, with five hundred men and boys to assist one, than it is to explore the private seas, the Atlantic and Pacific Ocean of one's being alone."

Sometimes meditation can be focused by using a "seed." The seed may be any object, thought, phrase, mantra, or diagram which you care to choose. It should be something simple, that's all.

Look at, or think about the object you have chosen. Try to be as fully here-now with it as you can. Willfully yet tranquilly ignore the messages which come unbidden into mentation. Concentrate your whole focus on this one thing and let all other objects be excluded from the field of consciousness. Do not think but pour your essence into it. Let your soul be your eyes.

The seed serves as a reference point. Your chief aim is to observe how mentation works without getting lost in it—to stay on top. The seed can help you observe how far away your mentation may go and it provides an anchor point to return to. Breathing can also serve as a valuable seed:

Try to attend to your breathing and nothing else for a time. Attend and be aware without any attempt to interfere or control your breathing. A valuable technique often used in Zen meditation is to count your breaths. Count "one" in inhalation, "two" on exhalation, and so on up to ten. Then begin over again at "one." See if you can stay here-now long enough to count three sets.

Another way to use breathing in meditation is to try to be without words while you inhale. Then, when you exhale let the words babble out. Even whisper the words if you are alone. Again, inhale while maintaining silence, exhale and let the words out. Practice. Don't expect immediate results.

As you concentrate on any seed you will find a dozen distractions, little chains of diversionary thoughts that will pull you away from the object time after time. You will be surprised and dismayed to see how many thoughts pull you in as many directions. "Got to take my clothes to the laundry." "Must call Mary Jane tonight." "Don't forget to return book to library."

"Oh, yes, buy that book on psychotherapy that John mentioned," and so on. It may seem as though you are never going to succeed to learn how your mind works and how to control it when you choose, but if you persist you will be pleased at your results in a short time. Thought trains may be sorted into three categories: helpful, unhelpful, and useless. Identify them at first and it will help you to be a witness apart from thinking, for you are the thinker, not the thoughts.

Sometimes when you come back to focus upon the seed, see if you can quiet your mind of internal babbling. See if you can attain internal silence. Don't mistake internal silence for blankness, trance, or "cessation of mind." Only talking will be absent, all other awarenesses persist.

It is not necessary to stop thought, only to stop internal talk. In fact it is not possible to stop thought absolutely without creating strain. Thought can be controlled, though, like the way one controls a stream of water by channeling it into fields for irrigation.

If you can still your surface-mind, if you can give yourself to one activity, simply looking at an object without reflective talk or self-consciousness, you will have a most fulfilling experience.

To reflect by thought is always to distort, and our minds are not good mirrors. To label is to pigeonhole and no matter how good the fit, there is always some loss. To leave the present is to pour out your energies elsewhere, usually accidentally and at random, entailing a loss for your own conscious ends.

Whereas to be truly with an object, to be fully here and now with a quiet mind means to use your energy for your own ends— oftentimes even to gain energy or tap some unknown source within you. Afterward you will feel peaceful and quietly alert, not tired or depressed. If that object of attention is your own self, your physical body, your emotions, and your ordinary mentation process, then the experience increases tenfold and your sense of serenity and togetherness will last for hours afterward.

When you can become quiet internally, detached from your mechanistic lower unconscious, then you may be able to contact your higher conscious mind. This is the first step in meditation. The second step is to bring back from the detached state something from your higher consciousness. As you meditate, form a desire that your higher consciousness will operate more fully within you during your ordinary daily activities.

If you continue to have trouble, and you undoubtedly will if you are normal, you might try these aids:

Write out what keeps coming into your mind as you attempt to focus on a simple object. Jot down everything that enters. Let as many unbidden thoughts come up as you possibly can, deliberately fantasize, daydream, plan future activities. Write down everything you have to do or think about, as well as whatever is of pressing interest, including urges to physical movement, and emotional states that may occur spontaneously now and then.

Perhaps such a purge will assist you to quiet your mind, and you can return tranquilly to your former object of meditation. You may find that the mere act of trying to suppress tangential thoughts and problems had made them loom larger than they actually were.

Another technique for getting into meditation is to turn your full attention to sense impressions merely as sense impressions, without regard to their significance. This may swamp the internal babbling and leave a little space in which you can reach out and expand your sense of self.

Do not strain to achieve focused meditation, awareness of mentation, or internal silence. If none of them come, let go a while, then try again. The truly quiet mind is passive, but in an active sense. It is relaxed the way a dancer or an athlete is relaxed while he moves in performance or action. He displays no unnecessary emotions, motions, or strains. Every muscle operates smoothly and efficiently with just enough tension to complete a movement gracefully. So too in meditation: there should be no unorganized and extraneous mental activity. After a while your thoughts will become aligned and focused without strain or effort.

We tend to believe the power to think is our natural right as human beings, but we are all too often tyrannized by automatic thinking, which enslaves our real selves. We do not recognize what is happening to us, as we are buffeted by random trains of thought and feeling like so many leaves in the wind. We seem helpless at first as "it" thinks. But if we observe "it" for a while, we may be able to attain control of our machinery. The mere act of making an effort to observe is the first step in regaining power for ourselves.

Much of what we call thinking consists of reveries and fantasies produced automatically by stimuli that are generated internally or impinge upon us from outside. We function like complex juke boxes; when a button is pushed we put on the corresponding record; part-way through, the reject button is pushed, and another button activates a different record. We all know people with whom we don't talk politics or religion or whom we never ask, "How's your health?" for we know we'll be forced to listen to records we've already heard a thousand times.

Try also to observe when the record-playing syndrome does not happen, as in some intense situation, or when some real and important problem forces us to be "with it" in order to succeed and survive.

If meditation does nothing more than help you align your mentation process, it will have done a great deal, for that is probably more than dozens of courses in economics, chemistry, mathematics, business, art, or psychology have ever done. When meditation becomes a habitual way of operating during the entire day, then the formal concentrated meditation period may be given up. Meditation will be of little permanent value though, if the major part of the day is spent in scattering thoughts idly over the landscape of your mental worlds. Once you've tried meditating, however, and now that you understand some of the ideas behind its practice, you will automatically be more aware of what happens to your "mental energy" during the day. You will realize right away whether you are gaining or losing energy and whether you are controlling your thoughts or being controlled by them.

Meditating, being here-now, and sensing the environment are all interwoven ways of being in the world and together they constitute a bootstrap operation for expanding and developing your consciousness. The exercises in all these chapters reinforce and complement each other. If you keep going back and retrying earlier exercises, you will derive different benefits from them as your understanding increases.

After you have practiced meditating for a while, you will probably begin to touch your higher consciousness more fully than you did in the intense here-now exercises of the previous chapters, and you may also find it easier to progress from the simple here-now to the transcendental here-now.

> The sage who by faith, devotion and meditation has realized the Self, and become one with Brahman, is released from the wheel of change and escapes from rebirth, sorrow and death.
>
> —*The Upanishads*

The Way of the Machines—Biofeedback Training

Controlled or not controlled?
The same dice shows two faces
Not controlled or controlled,
Both are a grievous error.

—*Zen Flesh, Zen Bones*

Background

Science constantly pushes into new frontiers. Beliefs, values, and superstitions must give way to experimental findings, predictable results, and, eventually, control. Now, even meditation and higher states of consciousness are being investigated as objectively and carefully as possible with the most sophisticated scientific instruments. For over thirty years researchers have measured electrical signals emanating from the brain itself. Four principal brain-wave frequencies have been named with Greek letters. The letters are assigned to the following frequency ranges.

Delta	0 — 3	cycles per second
		(also called "hertz")
Theta	4 — 7	cycles per second
Alpha	8 — 13	cycles per second
Beta	14 — 26	cycles per second

These frequencies occur in different mixtures during our waking and sleeping activities. In the waking state, with attention focused on the outside world, people usually produce mostly beta frequencies. If they close their eyes and think of nothing in particular they generally produce a mixture of alpha and beta. If they become drowsy and slip toward sleep, some theta frequencies often appear and there is less of alpha and beta. Delta waves are not normally present except in deep sleep. As more and more EEG experiments were done during the 1950s, it began to be apparent to researchers that there was a correspondence between the type of brain-wave pattern a person exhibited and the specific state of waking consciousness he was in. This new idea led some scientists to start thinking about the tales of strange states of "higher consciousness" supposedly attained in the Orient through the practice of certain meditative and physical exercises. If these states did exist, what sort of brain-wave patterns would their practitioners exhibit? This question led several investigators on expeditions to Asia and Japan in the 1950s and 1960s touting all manner of improvised portable EEG equipment. The results of their research are now world famous.

In their studies, they discovered that Zen monks, yogis, and other persons who practice meditation do in fact produce brain-wave patterns which are different from the average person's. While most people in the waking state exhibit irregular brain rhythms of varying frequencies, meditators produce even brain waves of one predominant frequency, the so-called alpha wave, a low voltage, sinusoidal wave, ranging from 8–13 cycles per second. Furthermore, while everyone produces the alpha brain-wave frequency some of the time, most people usually do so with less strength and regularity than do practiced meditators.

In 1958 Dr. Joe Kamiya, of the Langley Porter Neuropsychiatric Institute in San Francisco, found that most normal people could be trained to produce more alpha if they were given immediate feedback of their brain-wave patterns. He accomplished this by modifying electroencephalographic equipment to produce a tone whenever a person's brain produced alpha waves. The subjects kept trying different mental gymnastics until they succeeded in maintaining a steady tone. As expected, the best way to keep the tone on seemed to be equivalent to meditating, and "meditators" seemed to be able to learn more quickly to keep the tone on than nonmeditators.

Another biofeedback researcher, Dr. Lester G. Fehmi, of the State University of New York at Stony Brook, has noted that artists, athletes, and meditators seem to show more immediate "flexible control over EEG parameters" than average subjects.

As the pace of research continued, even some long-term Zen practitioners who tried brain-wave feedback equipment agreed that it might be useful in teaching people the fundamentals of meditation. Some commentators began predicting that science was on the way to perfecting "Instant Zen."

Opponents of the new technique argued that machines could not alter the consciousness of man, or if they could, that it was somehow cheating, like taking LSD to experience a mystical state, or riding a chair lift to the top of the ski hill. Perhaps the Puritan ethic runs deep. Or perhaps there is some fear of tampering with the most complicated structure in the known universe—the brain of man.

Whatever the feelings or fears, nothing is sacred to science, and research has continued rapidly in the last few years. Research is now being carried out in universities and laboratories all over the country. Entire scientific conferences are being devoted to this new field, called biofeedback training, and its implications, uses, and faults. Three basic hypotheses underlie the use of biofeedback techniques:

1. Any change in a person's psychological state (to an altered level of consciousness) is accompanied by a neurological or physiological change which can be measured.
2. The alteration of the appropriate neurological or physiological state will in turn be correlated with a corresponding change in psychological state.
3. Feedback training enables a person to alter his internal neurological or physiological state in any desired direction.

For many years yogis have been known to possess phenomenal control over their internal states. Some have dramatically lowered their heartbeat or even stopped their heart from pumping blood, have altered skin temperature, or markedly changed their brain rhythms. But whether these neurophysiological states are causally related to achieving a higher state of consciousness or whether they are merely minor by-products or side effects is not fully understood.

It had heretofore been assumed that bodily functions normally controlled by the autonomic nervous system could not be brought under conscious control. The advent of biofeedback has shown this assumption to be false. With proper instrumentation and training procedures practically every autonomic function can be modified to some degree by conscious will.

Thus, hypothesis number three is definitely confirmed; people can learn to control or modify their internal neurological or physiological states. At first it may seem bizarre that a person can lower or raise his heartbeat or his skin temperature or produce alpha brain waves just by his will, but if we look at the principle it is already familiar to us (though still a mystery). We learn control of brain waves in the same fashion that we learn anything else. The highly complex skills performed by our arms and hands, for example, are first attempted as rather gross bodily movements. By observing these movements we obtain visual feedback and refine them to whatever degree of accuracy or control we desire—be it typing or twiddling our thumbs. We learn, in short, by feedback—from our external and internal environment as perceived through our sense receptors. There are over 2000 feedback systems in the human body—without feedback we would literally "become unglued,"as the kids say nowadays. I can't tell you how to move your arm or how to be here and now in what you are doing, or how to produce alpha waves. You have to make the efforts and pay attention to the feedback. How you actually do it, how you direct the complex machinery of the brain or body cannot be answered in current scientific terms. Nevertheless, you alter your brain's electrical waves every time you initiate any action or thought.

Control is perhaps too strong a word for what happens in biofeedback training. Rather, there must be a "gentle allowing," a kind of "relaxing into it," or what has been termed "passive volition." One gives one's body the command and stands aside while it happens. Control versus not-control seems to be linguistic dichotomy, as far as internal states are concerned. For who's controlling whom when brain waves are altered?

Instrumentation and Research Findings

I had been designing and marketing portable, inexpensive psychological instruments since 1960 and when I heard of Kamiya's work in 1966, I designed the Alpha Sensor for brain-wave training. Since then about thirty companies have been marketing brain-wave equipment and the field promises to become a big industry in the next few years. The instruments we are developing now at PsychoPhysics Labs are like electronic eyes which see into the body. They signal what is happening in the form of lights that wink or tones that sound. For example, I designed and patented an instrument that measures skin resistance (called the Relaxometer) which uses two conducting cloth electrodes that wrap around the finger tips. The instrument then generates a base tone which changes in pitch as a person's skin resistance changes. The more excited he gets, the higher the pitch. As he relaxes the pitch lowers. This signal is indicative of the activity of the sympathetic branch of the autonomic nervous system. By giving the person feedback on this measure, he can readily see how different psychological or physiological stimuli affect him. He can practice with different emotions and see how his autonomic nervous system reacts; he can induce feelings of anxiety or anger, then calmness, tranquillity, or love. He can experiment with muscle tension, relaxation, deep breathing, or a dozen other parameters and hear a correlate of his own reactions.

Skin resistance is one of the most sensitive measures of emotional reaction and it has been used for many years in all lie-detection equipment. It has also been used as an adjunct to various kinds of psychotherapy, to help the patient and the therapist know when they touch on "sensitive" areas which need further investigation.

For example; Dianetics and Scientology, as developed by L. Ron Hubbard, make extensive use of a very sensitive skin-resistance device, called an E-meter, in their therapy, which is called auditing. The GSR device is used by an auditor to establish a more effective communication with his patients. By watching the needle on his meter, the Auditor can actually "see" emotionally charged thoughts keying in and out of his patient's mind—often at a level just below the conscious awareness of the patient himself. This allows him to aid his patient to bypass the usual defense mechanisms and to quickly zero in on those areas which it is most important for him to work on. Thus, with the help of a biofeedback device to extend the perception of the therapist, it has been possible to develop a counseling technology which is considerably faster and more efficient than the traditional forms of psychotherapy and psychoanalysis. Whatever one may think about Scientology as a religion or cult, this particular technique works. It has been effectively used by traditional psychotherapists as well as Scientology auditors.

In general, all biofeedback instruments work in about the same way: electrodes pick up the signals from the body which are then modified electronically to produce visual, auditory, or even tactile feedback. The person trying to learn autonomic or brain control, guides his behavior by the feedback. Sooner or later he's successful. One of the latest brain-wave monitors I have developed, called the Bio-Feedback Trainer, uses cloth electrodes to pick up microvolt signals from the scalp. After amplification, the desired brain wave is electronically filtered from the many frequencies of brain waves present and used to modulate a tone generator within the Bio-Feedback Trainer. Either alpha or theta can be selected from the brain waves.

Each cycle of the alpha waves produces an audible beep from the machine and the louder the beep, the stronger the amplitude of the alpha wave. The object is to try to maintain a steady stream of beeps and to increase their loudness. Most subjects find that they can learn to do this quite easily with relatively little practice. Moreover, when they do succeed in producing a continuous stream of loud beeps, they usually report a definite and corresponding change in their state of consciousness. In a recent paper (unpublished as of May 1972) Dr. Fehmi reports on some subjects' description of this state:

> The alpha experience is frequently described as an "increase in smooth flowing energy, a release of tension and a spreading of

attentional focus" which is maintained while alpha is present. The alpha experience is arrested when the subjects adopt a critical objective attitude toward something.

Alpha has generally been associated with relaxed wakefulness. . . . Subjects report that while producing alpha, they attend more effortlessly, more flexibly and more diffusely to either internal or external stimuli than they do during the production of other types of brain rhythms. While producing alpha, their perceptions are inclined toward integrating larger gestalts; they appear more expansive and more accepting of the objects of their attention. . . . Some subjects who have been given training only in increasing alpha activity and who at the beginning of training, were reserved and circumspect, behave light-heartedly and more openly after bio-feedback training.

. . . a frequent observation by subjects, after some hours of training exclusively devoted to alpha production, is that they get along with people better than before training. Their friends do not readily identify any specific change, but report that interactions are more pleasant and free. These reports suggest that an increase in attentional flexibility accrues with successful alpha training.

These findings concur with my own observations of myself and others. When I react to events and strains of the business day with tensions and irritation I can attach an Alpha Sensor and after ten or fifteen minutes return refreshed and tranquil to work.

Scientific papers are appearing at an enormous rate in this new field and this is no place to review them, but here's a sampling of some recent findings:

1. At Harvard University Medical School a group of college students were trained in less than one hour to slow their heart rates by an average of nine beats a minute.

2. Chronic headaches were relieved in several persons by teaching them to control their forehead skin temperature. This work was supervised by Dr. Elmer Green of the Menninger Foundation. One woman learned to raise her hand temperature ten degrees in two and a half minutes simply by thinking about it. Temperature control really means control of blood flow. This may be extremely useful for helping

infected areas to heal, to stop bleeding, or aiding muscles to perform better under stress.

3. Indirect relaxation of muscles constitutes another area where biofeedback equipment has been successfully applied. By placing electrodes on muscles that cause certain kinds of headaches when chronically tensed, Dr. Hans Stoyva of the University of Colorado Medical School has allowed people to be more vividly aware of their muscle tensions than ordinarily possible. With such awareness they have learned to relax tense muscles thereby dramatically easing the pain.

4. Dr. Elmer Green at the Menninger Foundation reports that there seems to be a correlation between memory effectiveness and percentage alpha. He tested the memory of several students whom he trained to increase the percentage of eyes-open alpha. He found that their ability to remember was correlated with the percentage of alpha waves present while they were trying to remember. It is his feeling that ". . . an alpha training program might be of great value in assisting students to overcome 'mental blocks' during examinations."

5. Dr. Green has found what may be a relationship between the theta brain-wave state (4–7 cps) and creativity. ". . . the physiological state associated with theta contained, in a number of subjects, very clear hypnagogic-like imagery. Pictures or ideas would spring full blown into consciousness without the person being aware of their creation. The theta 'reverie,' as we began to call it, was definitely different from a daydreaming state and much to our surprise we found that it seemed to correspond with descriptions given by geniuses of the past of the state of consciousness they experienced while being their most creative."

6. At the State University of New York at Stony Brook, Dr. Lester G. Fehmi has reported a correspondence between subjects' ability to concentrate and certain types of brain waves. Dr. Fehmi has been studying the phase agreement of EEG activity simultaneously recorded from different electrode placements on the brain. He has found that when the alpha rhythms recorded from the right and left occipital lobes were within fifteen degrees of being in phase, the subjects report ". . . a relatively stable mental image" and a "one-pointedness of mental focus." Moreover when the subjects are taught to increase

the amplitude of their alpha activity while maintaining the phase agreement, they demonstrate the ability to maintain an intense concentration without tension for prolonged periods, a talent evidenced by few people other than Zen masters.

7. A particularly interesting phenomenon reported recently from many laboratories is that subjects who have undergone brain-wave training in lab experiments tend to show an increase in their baseline alpha and theta readings even after their experimental sessions have ceased. This finding aligns with other reports that Zen and yogic and other meditators enjoy higher alpha and theta baselines than most people not regularly engaged in these disciplines. This is a very interesting finding since high alpha and theta baselines tend to be correlated with relaxation, mental alertness, and creativity. It appears that the regular use of a brain-wave training device may produce desirable changes in a person's mental state that extend considerably beyond the times he actually uses the device.

8. Ten persons were given one hour a day training on simultaneous alpha and theta control by Dr. Green of the Menninger Foundation. Their instructions were to increase theta waves and decrease alpha waves. Prior to each daily session, they were given eight minutes of autogenic training (a relaxation technique) and five minutes of slow breathing.

After five weeks of the planned ten-week training program, half of the people in the program reported definite differences in their perception of the world or themselves. Statements such as: "I feel more put together now" or "Colors seem different to me now" reflect some of their changed states. At the time of this writing (April 1972) the study is not complete, but so far the results seem highly positive.

The above results indicate that in the near future people will more and more be using biofeedback equipment instead of, or in addition to, drugs for all kinds of psychosomatic ailments arising from nervous tension or unbalanced living. Moreover, the possibilities are real that biofeedback training will soon be used to help people increase their powers of concentration and to enhance their creative potential.

Higher States of Consciousness

While observations indicate that Zen monks and yogis produce copious theta waves as well as alpha waves, people who have learned to produce these waves via biofeedback instruments, or people who naturally produce them already, do not necessarily experience transcendental states of consciousness. However, as described earlier, most people who learn to increase their alpha and theta production by biofeedback training, do report some change in their subjective state of consciousness. Thus, hypothesis number two appears to be confirmed. In order to experience any kind of change of perceptions or consciousness a person needs to roughly double his present alpha or theta baseline.

With regard to higher states of consciousness, it may be that we do not yet know precisely what a person's neurological or physiological correlates are. Alpha and theta rhythms may be only casual side effects or a necessary but not sufficient condition for attaining higher states of consciousness. Perhaps the final key lies in some measurements we can't conveniently make with our present technology—such as hormone secretions from the pituitary gland or the pineal gland. Or, perhaps, there is some special combination of the four major brain waves, some musical chord that must be struck before a man can enter a more conscious state. In this respect, Dr. Elmer Green has devised an auditory feedback system in which ". . . beta waves are made to produce a piccolo type of music. Alpha sounds like a flute, theta like an oboe, and delta like a bassoon." Using devices like this, it may be possible to isolate the exact musical symphonies associated with specific higher states and then train people to produce them. On the other hand, perhaps higher consciousness truly lies beyond the power of present scientific investigation, but we can't know until we try. Who can predict what valuable discoveries may lie before us?

People who get into alpha states using biofeedback instruments consistently report a feeling of relaxation and well-being. When using the Bio-Feedback Trainer I feel like the cotton is pulled out of my head, leaving a clear space. Anxieties, problems, and other tensions seem to melt away, leaving me with a sense of relief and peace. Alpha production is definitely in the same direction as that produced by meditation for me at least, and like meditation, the after effect is one of being more centered, calm, and collected. After working with the instrument for a few days, I no longer regularly need it to get into the same state, but it helps to use it now and then for focus and as a way of keeping myself honest.

Using a Bio-Feedback Trainer is not "cheating" or artificially forcing the brain to perform in any way. It merely shortcuts my here-now process of attending to my thoughts. When I meditate, trying to be here-now with my mentation process, I sometimes get caught up by a thought train and lose my detachment from it. With the Bio-Feedback Trainer chirping, I have an external reminder that my mentation process has altered. So long as I am detached, the sound of the instrument is present and fairly steady. When I come down a little bit, the alpha pattern often becomes irregular.

In testing hundreds of people, I have observed tremendous individual variations which do not always correspond to variations in apparent level of consciousness. I have come across a number of very ordinary people who generate alpha and theta waves like Zen monks, yet these people had no interest or desire in reaching any altered state of consciousness or did they appear to possess any abilities or perceptions out of the ordinary. They were not especially able to be present to their immediate surroundings or were they tuned into any transcendental state.

For this reason I do not think that making alpha or theta waves is a sufficient condition for attaining a more highly conscious state. Furthermore, children between three and six produce alpha and theta waves readily yet they are not necessarily superaware beings. They are, however, much closer to their essence than most adults, and they are more creative.

Just the same, alpha production *may* be necessary to achieving an altered state of consciousness. In fact, it may be a prerequisite for proper use of the brain. For example, alpha training has been found helpful in certain types of learning improvement. As with autohypnosis or autosuggestion, people in alpha are more open to programing alterations in their postsession behavior, a factor which may be helpful in drug rehabilitation and alcoholism. By learning to produce alpha while using the machine, persons suffering from anxiety or other problems may be able to go into alpha during the day, when they are troubled, without needing the machine. The calm feeling generated along with alpha waves enables them to view their problems in a more detached manner.

The majority of people produce some alpha just by closing their eyes. Merely to produce alpha is nothing special. Functioning while one is in the alpha state (or theta, or both) is the key to behavioral change or improved learning or whatever one is trying to accomplish. Perhaps entering the alpha state is analogous to entering a room with many doors. Once in that place, many possibilities are open to one.

Jose Silva has been actively teaching people to expand their mental abilities while they are relaxed and generally in an alpha state. Many of his students report dramatic experiences of extrasensory perception, especially of the internal states of health of other persons. This corresponds to my own similiar experiences of extrasensory awareness of the states of other persons, and I frequently use this in my therapeutic practice to help me understand what might be bothering a person. I close my eyes, relax my body, visualize an image of the person, ask a question about him or her, and wait for some kind of answer, picture, or thought. This kind of "intuition" is commonly used by many people, although perhaps only in a random or haphazard fashion.

Some researchers have suggested that alpha training may enhance the learning of languages, for when a person is in the alpha state he is more attentive to stimuli. Some exciting work in this area is being carried on behind the Iron Curtain, especially in Czechoslovakia. The interested reader is referred to *Psychic Discoveries Behind the Iron Curtain*, by Shroeder and Ostrander, for additional details on this research.

Why is all this possible? What's going on in the brain during the production of alpha or theta waves? How is this related to being here-now? How could it possibly be related to a higher state of consciousness? As yet, we do not know. Perhaps when the brain is in alpha, more neurons fire in a synchronized fashion; i.e., the brain becomes more organized. Normally, many different frequencies occur at the same time. A discordant condition exists. During the production of alpha the higher frequencies diminish or die away completely. We might literally say that a person is "more together." Perhaps the brain is more receptive to commands, to sensory input, or to learning anything.

The brain (and body) may be likened to an amplifier through which our essence or higher consciousness operates. This amplifier system is turned on, since we are alive and functioning, but seldom properly tuned or adjusted. Hence we waste nervous and mental energy, are unable to discipline ourselves, cannot work consistently, and do not possess any "real will."

Moreover, whatever thoughts we put into our brain amplifier or whatever thoughts are put in from outside by our parents, teachers, or general cultural milieu are amplified willy-nilly. In a neurological sense, we construct our own reality. For the most

minute thoughts become amplified into patterns of muscle'
tension, into actions, further thoughts, and so on. As we interact
with the external world, and with the action of others, we modify
these actions and take in new thoughts which in turn become
amplified. Worries and negative thoughts or self-criticisms may
often turn into self-fulfilling prophecies. We have to be careful
what we feed our computer brains with, and how we program
our children's. Generally there is little conscious direction to our
thoughts; we just let them happen. We seldom act; we mostly
react against the buffets of life. Alpha training, meditation, or
simply being here-now quiets us and permits more of our actions
to be directed from our higher self rather than being mere
re-actions mechanically carried out in response to external stimuli
or the prodding of others. Biofeedback training tunes up the brain
and makes it more useful as an instrument for the higher
consciousness. Perhaps it is analogous to reducing the noise level
(beta frequencies) of an amplifier, thereby improving the
receptivity of the instrument.

With these procedures of training we can keep above the daily
barrage of stimuli; we can keep on top of things. Once we are
detached and able to tune up our brain computer-amplifier, we
can program it as we choose. We create our own future anyway,
so we might as well tune up our minds to be happy or to
achieve our goals, rather than let them be made up at random
for us. Otherwise our mental computer will attend to random
information, not helping us much at all.

In our normal condition, our energies are scattered and
unorganized. We sometimes have the feeling that things are
working against us. Perhaps each separate subpersonality to
which we say "I" operates with a slightly different portion or
circuit of the brain. One "I" can't recall where another "I" put
something, or what another "I" said. Our friends perceive us as
absent-minded, hypocritical, liars, unorganized, or scatterbrained.

And probably we are—at least my behavior seems that way at times, even to me! Generally we function as badly managed computers—a tangle of conditioned responses and acquired personalities. It may be that we are operating from different brain hemispheres at different times. Perhaps brain operation switches randomly back and forth from one hemisphere to the other. In our laboratory, we are currently designing a unit to provide phase-training or coordination between the two hemispheres. It remains to be seen what use this feedback instrument will have, but to date the findings seem positive and beneficial.

Getting into the alpha state, meditating, or being here-now with the external world really helps in getting our heads together. After that, what we do depends on what we set for our goals.

At the time of this writing, we do not know how best to consciously increase alpha brain rhythms. It is not a matter of willful control, but rather a gentle allowing, an attunement to one of the brain's rhythms. The following exercise (similar to one given in the previous chapter) has proved useful as a starter:

> **Sit quietly and proceed throughout your body with an inner focus of attention. Wherever there are tense areas relax them by first tensing them hard, then letting go. Let your attention wander systematically over your entire body. Pay special attention to your face and the muscles around your mouth and eyes. Go around your neck, working up and down the muscles running from the scalp to the shoulders.**

This exercise is a useful one before beginning any important activity, either mental or physical. Here is one which I have found useful for initial alpha training:

> **With eyes open, inhale a nice easy breath. As you exhale, gently close your eyes. Accompany this by a kind of mental sigh—a letting go of everything.**

This will often produce a short burst of alpha, and by repeating it a number of times you will be able to get the "feel" of the alpha state and, hopefully, increase its duration.

Another simple technique that may be useful is to:

Imagine something very pleasant or take an imaginary trip to a beautiful place. Imagine yourself soaking in the warm sunshine or floating in warm water. After you get comfortable in your imaginary place, do not visualize your surroundings. Let auditory and tactile sensations preside.

Visualization often blocks alpha. When you first become proficient at producing alpha, you may learn that you can stop and start it (with your eyes closed) by visualizing or not visualizing some image. If this is the case for you, practice clear imagery until you have good concentration and control.

Alpha has been clearly shown to be related to the visual part of the brain, although all the details are not yet known. A strong light may be used to help induce alpha even through closed eyelids. Some brain-wave instruments have provision for attaching a light for visual feedback of the alpha. You may find this useful. I do not recommend the use of a regular strobe light as the intense beam may harm the eyes or cause epilepticlike seizures. However, a strobe control for incandescent lights is available from my company, Biofeedback Instruments, Inc., which will not harm the eyes. You may find this device useful for inducing alpha or for lowering it to the theta band.

Set the blink frequency to the alpha frequency and let the light shine through your closed eyelids. If you can produce alpha, try gradually decreasing the blink rate of the light to see if your alpha will be lowered into the theta range of 4–7cps.

Some people have reported alpha enhancement by listening to a ten-cycle beeping tone. You can generate this tone with an

incandescent strobe unit or by taping the chirping of a
Bio-Feedback Trainer onto a tape loop.

Breathing techniques affect alpha production, but most of these
should be done under supervision of an experienced teacher.
One that you may try without danger consists of simply slowing
the breath.

> **Sit quietly and breathe as slowly as you comfortably can. When
> you have fully inhaled, immediately begin to exhale slowly. At
> the bottom of the expiration cycle, again begin an easy and very
> slow inhalation. Try to change from one cycle to the other with a
> very minimum of disturbance or jerkiness. Try to breathe as
> slowly as possible.**

U.S. Andersen describes many fascinating aspects of
alpha-wave training and related disciplines for expanding
consciousness in his book, *The Greatest Power in the Universe*.
He reports inducing alpha waves by using a vibrator or massage
device which he set at alpha frequency and applied to various
parts of the body where chronic tensions were present.

In my research I am exploring other aspects of biofeedback
training which might be of value. You may duplicate some of this
work with the Bio-Feedback Trainer or other biofeedback
equipment.

> **Connect your wrist electrodes to the alpha sensor. Sit quietly,
> listening to the lub-dub sound generated by the heart. Then begin
> to synchronize your breathing to the heart rate. There are four
> parts to the breath cycle—inspiration, hold in; expiration, hold
> out. For each part, count a definite number of heartbeats. You
> should experiment to find your own natural count, but try
> something like 7, 5, 7, 5 for a start.**

Synchronization of heart rate with breathing does not ordinarily
occur in the course of our daily living. I find it extremely pleasant

and a wonderful way to begin meditation or alpha training. Anyone can do this exercise because it takes no great effort.

A more difficult exercise involves synchronization of alpha brain waves and heartbeat. To do this, I connect one electrode to the wrist and one to the back of the head. The "lub-dub" pulse of the heart will be heard superimposed upon the "beep-beep" of the Bio-Feedback Trainer. When synchronized, the sounds merge in a way that is difficult to verbalize, but easy to hear. As far as I know, this is an unexplored area of biofeedback training.

The activity of the sympathetic nervous system, a barometer of emotional activity, can also be integrated with brain-wave activity.

Connect the relaxometer or audible psychogalvanometer to the fingers of one hand at the same time that you are connected to the Bio-Feedback Trainer. Switch your attention back and forth from the sound of the relaxometer to the alpha beeps and try to lower the relaxometer pitch as you produce alpha. What can you observe? Experiment with the yogic locks or various meditation procedures as you listen to the feedback from both instruments.

I do not know exactly how the sympathetic nervous-system activity relates to the central nervous system or the brain rhythms. Although studies are now being undertaken, it may be some time before any answers are found. It only seems natural, however, that some synchronization of the sympathetic with the central nervous system is not only possible but desirable.

Theta waves are harder to produce than alpha and are generally not produced when the eyes are open. To get into theta, try sinking into a state of reverie. Let yourself go without fear of holding on. It's better to use an instrument produced by Bio-Feedback Instruments, "the Alpha-Theta Synchronizer," which allows you to hear both alpha and theta simultaneously. Then try to maintain some alpha while you gradually learn to produce theta. Doing this helps keep one somewhat alert and able to remember what happens while in the theta state. At the present time, research on theta is even more tentative than research on alpha; but all indications so far indicate that beneficial results may be obtained by those who can increase their theta waves.

Perhaps the human organism may be considered analogous to a symphony orchestra, consisting of a multitude of energies and vibrations. However, under ordinary conditions of living, the organism is seldom properly tuned, integrated, or organized, and it operates in a rather random, erratic fashion. Meditation, chanting, ritual dancing, and other specialized exercises are designed to tune the organism. Brain-wave training, as I mentioned before, seems to be another way of tuning the brain rhythms so that the body and emotions, as well as the mind, may be able to work together.

Assuming that this is possible, the obvious next step will be to synchronize one's heartbeat and/or alpha with another person's. With the Bio-Feedback Trainer this can be done by attaching one electrode to one person and the second electrode to the other person, then completing the circuit by holding moistened hands or otherwise making body contact. Research in this area is just beginning.

Brain-wave synchronization between two persons may be a prerequisite for telepathy, and research on this looks promising. U.S. Andersen, an independent biofeedback researcher, reports a successful experiment wherein the receiver was in alpha and the sender in theta.

Psychokinesis, or the ability to move objects by mind effects alone, has been associated with high front-to-back brain-wave activity in at least one instance. So far, though, no one has been able to train himself to produce such specialized brain activity.

Perhaps psychokinesis requires some subtle "tuning" of brain rhythms to objects in the external world or some resonance effect not yet discovered.

As a science, biofeedback training is in its infancy. No one knows where it will lead. At the present time its techniques look very promising for improving the health of many people. A number of psychosomatic diseases will respond to some form of feedback training, given a motivated subject. There is no doubt that biofeedback training can help people relax, concentrate, improve their recall, attention span, enhance their creativity, or otherwise function more ably in the world. It is just as true, however, that people could be helped by autogenic training, self-hypnosis, meditation, or all the ordinary forms of psychoanalysis and psychotherapy. It is also the case that if a person begins to function better in his ordinary activities, then the pathway to the higher consciousness within him is made easier. Perhaps it is Western man's unique cultural milieu that gives him extra faith in machines. Or perhaps it is the case that machines will prove more efficacious than the old established guru-disciple method of altering consciousness. The truth remains to be determined. We stand at the threshold of new discoveries.

> The great path has no gates,
> Thousands of roads enter it.
> When one passes through this gateless gate
> He walks freely between heaven and earth.
>
> —*Zen Flesh, Zen Bones*

| VII |

Essence and Personality

The man who has learned the Self is separate from the
body, the senses, and the mind, and has fully known him,
the soul of truth, the subtle principle—such a man verily
attains to him, and is exceeding glad, because he has found
the source and dwelling place of all felicity. The Self, whose
symbol is OM, is the omniscient Lord. He is not born. He
does not die. He is neither cause nor effect. This Ancient
One is unborn, imperishable, eternal: though the body be
destroyed, he is not killed. Smaller than the smallest, greater
than the greatest, this Self forever dwells within the hearts of
all. When a man is free from desire, his mind and senses
purified, he beholds the glory of the Self and is without
sorrow. Having given up the false identification of the Self
with the senses and the mind, and knowing the Self to be
Brahman, the wise, on departing this life, becomes immortal.

—The Upanishads

Most of what we do, say, write, or think does not originate
within us, but is borrowed from parents, teachers, friends and all
the mass culture around us—radio, television, movies,
newspapers, and books. We absorb all manner of facts, beliefs,
attitudes, values, opinions, likes, and dislikes about everyone and

everything, including ourselves, the same way we put on clothes. Unlike clothes, however, such likes and dislikes, once put on, are seldom discarded.

Beneath this potpourri of personalities and external traits lies our essence, the core of our being. When we are honestly present to our surroundings with a mind free from the entrapments of memories, words, or fantasies, or when the mind is stilled in meditation, transcendental essence emerges. Essence is that sparkle of elemental life force, that inner light which glows in every human being. Essence forms the eternal part of us, personality the ephemeral. Our characteristic disposition and temperament, our unique way of organizing the impressions of the moment, relating to the world and to others flows from essence, but is shaped, modulated, or even entirely dominated by our acquired personalities.

In each of us, these two components—personality and essence —are manifest in varying degrees throughout our lives. When we are infants, essence predominates; as we mature we acquire our personalities, learn a language, and develop ways of thinking and behaving which slowly mold our character and may obscure our essence altogether. Although acquired behavior may be necessary for the survival of our organism, it can become mechanical and automatic.

Without quite being aware of it, we lose some of our freedom when we acquire a personality. Or, to put it another way, we lose our real selves, our inner essence. Most people think that what they believe, say, write, or do in each instance is truly and originally their own. Even negative and unpleasant traits and mannerisms are held on to, as though they were one's personal property. Yet, deep inside, our essence struggles to reveal itself, so we feel an undefined sense of unreality in our lives. Only in rare moments of insight do we realize that something is not right, that we have no true freedom. Sometimes we have vague feelings of nostalgia which come from longing to shed our unreal, acquired personalities and return to essence, but we do not know how.

It is not too difficult to recontact essence and let its glow back into your life. The exercises in this chapter are specifically designed to help separate essence from personality and get you started on a new track. Once the work is begun, you can probably continue it on your own.

Of course, essence and personality are not totally separable aspects of a human being, or is one the real and the other artificial. Essence and personality are merely terms for different aspects of our total make-up. There exists no human of pure essence, although there are humans who live almost entirely as mechanical personalities. If you wish to observe the essence-aspect of human nature, watch young children, about the age of two, before they have been too much exposed to parents, teachers, rules, and requirements—before they have learned to build walls around their essence. You will see essence bubbling up with every childish squeal, with every hop, skip, or jump of delight. Children express their real selves from wakeup time to sleeptime, if we let them. Watch and you will see these children pulling at you and at other adults, trying hard to pull your essence into being along with theirs. Have you not felt it?

Have you seen, too, those few, those very few people whose essence shines out from their eyes, shines out sometimes with such force that it is both painful and embarrassing to be in their presence? The presence of such people threatens our sham personalities, but if we can let go of our personalities—even temporarily—it can be a joyful experience.

In most adults you can observe the workings of an acquired personality. For many, the older they become, the more mechanically they live. Essence, that inner self basic to real communication, is entirely covered—no spark remains. The only things that issue forth are canned speeches and reflexes to suit every occasion. In extreme cases, we call it senility, a kind of predeath has already set in. Look about you. Look at the "organization man," look at the politician, the college professor, the policeman. Look at any man, woman, or child over the age of five. Look into their eyes. What do you see? Look into the mirror.

Most of the time, most of us live by means of our acquired personalities. Occasionally, the superficial thought patterns in which we are molded can be pushed aside or stilled. This may happen when we meditate or concentrate with our whole attention on some sound or sight, or when we engage in some deeply absorbing task. When we are fully here and now, there is no room for mechanical behavior. Each situation is unique and our awareness of it must uniquely match it. When this happens, personality may be temporarily cast away and we can become more alive, more ourselves.

Sometimes, by chance, experiences combine in just the right way with some inner state. Essence resonates strongly and personality fades away. We look at something—maybe something commonplace, maybe something extraordinarily dramatic—or we move in a certain way, or we talk to a certain person—and we feel a strange uplifting sense of wonder. For a brief instant, a minute, an hour, or even a whole day, we are vividly aware of our inner self or essence. We become filled with a sense of peace, and inner time seems to stand still. When we return to our ordinary state, we retain a vivid memory of the richer self within.

These happenings, which Abraham Maslow terms peak-experiences, and Zen teaching calls satori, occur now and then in even the most tedious of lives.

You may have already experienced such states as you did the exercises in the previous chapters. Being here and now with the world puts one directly in touch with essence and through essence, with a higher state of consciousness. Meditating leads one to the same place by an inner route.

Love is one of the strongest forces capable of penetrating superficial layers of personality and uncovering essence. I mean the state that is experienced when one looks and looks into another's eyes and sees one's self and the other and the world, deeper and deeper, until there is nothing and there is everything and here is now and now is forever. Love is that strange psychedelic potion, which produces its own "high," its own euphoric state of expanded consciousness. Love pulls essence into being, in all but the most rigid and covert of us. If you have deeply loved, then you have known essence. May you always know it.

For most of us, unfortunately, love seldom exists as a permanent state. We soon lapse into habitual behavior, and ritualize our loving and our living without examining the origins and patterns of these rituals. Society has set up certain rules for our conduct which we blindly follow. Our daily behavior is prescribed by "thou shalts" and "thou shalt not's": eat this way, dress that way, move this way, think that way, and so on.

Essence is buried under the surface ebb and flow of attitudes, beliefs, prejudices, and trivia—under the sea of information which threatens to submerge us. The medium does more than massage us; it covers us drop by drop, bit by bit, layer by layer until essence is lost, like the seed of a hailstone that has been tossed from cloud to cloud until, at last, encrusted and weighted with ice, it falls to the earth.

One of the most subtle forms of influence lies in the language which we use; a language which we are not responsible for, but which we are forced to learn and use for most of our thinking and communication. Benjamin Lee Whorf was one of the first linguists to see the structure of our language for the prison that it is.

. . . thinking also follows a network of tracks laid down in a given language, an organization which may concentrate systematically upon certain phases of reality, certain aspects of intelligence, and may systematically discard others featured by other languages. The individual is utterly unaware of this organization and is constrained completely within its unbreakable bonds. This organization is imposed from outside the narrow circle of the personal consciousness, making of that consciousness a mere puppet. Linguistic maneuverings are held in unsensed and unbreakable bonds of patterns . . . scientist and yokel, scholar and tribesman, all use their personal consciousness in the same dim-witted sort of way, as unaware of the beautiful and inexorable systems that control them as a cowherd is of cosmic rays.*

We can learn to undo many of these imposed linguistic bonds which fetter the expression of our personality, but only when we become aware of them. Chapter II's exercises on internal silence may effectively halt linguistically conditioned thought patterns. The following additional exercises will also help provide you with a check on unconscious rituals, habits, and customs:

Take a notebook to your next meal. As you start to eat consider exactly what you are going to do. How do you sit? Where do you sit? Carefully, in thought, go over every minute aspect of the meal. What foods are served? How are they prepared and why are they prepared that way? How will you eat them? With what tools? With what condiments? In what order? Try to write down in your notebook those aspects of mealtime activities which are not acquired through learning, habit, usage, or outdated beliefs.

You may have a difficult time finding any aspects. Go on to tackle the area of clothing.

Stop right now and consider your clothes. Start from your feet up, and ask yourself, which of the many articles you are wearing are ones that you truly chose to wear and which were chosen because of other people or for other reasons?

*Language, Thought, and Reality, M.I.T. Press, 1956 (pp. 256–257).

You will probably observe that many of your clothes were acquired out of compliance with other people, or with social customs. Given complete freedom, you might very well dress differently. Can you seriously imagine what you might wear if you were perfectly free?

Much of what we do, say, and think serves to satisfy others in some direct or indirect fashion. In the same way that we put on clothes, we imitate others in our manner of speech and thought. Furthermore, thoughts and actions, like ready-made clothes, are usually only available in certain standard forms and sizes. If we want to dress differently, we have to make many of our own clothes and this involves some hard work. If we want to think or act differently, we have to shape our own thoughts and this, too, is hard work.

As an exercise, extend your analysis of clothes and clothing to a day's activities:

> **Take just one hour at a time, on successive days, and try to record all the things that you do. Note how many of them are mechanically done, to satisfy some vague notions about how others might judge you. How many of them are done to satisfy directly some real other person? How many of them are done because you yourself want to do them that way, at that particular time and place? How many things can you find that you do during the day which are not or have not been acquired from somewhere else? What do you do just for you?**

If you observe your inner state as you do different things, you may realize how often you feel forced to do something you do not really want to do. Each time this happens you lose a little energy wrangling with yourself, creating more strains and tensions in your body, and murdering your inner essence bit by bit.

How many times a day do you say to yourself: "I feel this way but I shouldn't," or "I have to eat now," or "I must read this book"? How many times a day do you say: "I want to do this—just for me"? Can we become more sensitive to what the organism itself wants to do, how it wants to move, and what its most basic emotions and feelings are? Alan W. Watts points out that we are induced by our language forms and the process of socialization to believe that a separate "will" or "conscious self" controls the organism. What we do not see is that this false personality often works against the biological organism. This "conscious self" is an internalization of the social demands placed upon us, coupled with the role we have been assigned by parents, teachers, and early associations. By means of this artificial social personality, Watts says, we learn to control ourselves and conform to the requirements of social life, but we pay a heavy price for these social privileges. Furthermore, this artificial outer self exists not as a single entity, but as a complex of selves. Everybody has a family, social, racial, and national self as well as biological and physical self. The social self in turn is often divisible into several more subselves. Although such divisions are artificial, they can be worthwhile learning aids. If you attempt to observe your outer subselves from a higher vantage point you will come much closer to knowing your inner self or essence. Ultimately, a voluntary reintegration should be possible, but meanwhile some useful work can be done.

When you split yourself into parts the term "I" is no longer meaningful. Try substituting the word "here" or "it" as illustrated in the following exercise.

Whenever you are possessed by a strong dislike or like or whenever you have an impulse to do something, try to disassociate it from you. Instead of saying "I want to leave," say "Here is leaving." Or, if you feel angry, do not say "I am angry," but try saying "Here is angering," or "It is angering."

This is an exercise, not necessarily a way of living, to help you disengage yourself from aspects of your behavior that you have uncritically incorporated from your social environment. Don't make this exercise into some sort of serious and onerous task. Make a game out of it. Play with your wishes and wants by pretending that they are not really yours. Try to get one up on yourself and observe what is going on. Experiment to see how many different ways you can reformulate likes and dislikes, so as to disassociate yourself from them and get an objective look at them. Observe what feelings come up when you reformulate situations in impersonal terms. You might sort out your genuine desires from those which are only acquired. After you practice saying "here" or "it" for a while, then "I" will come to have a real meaning.

The little word "I" hides so much complexity! We think it refers to a single and separate being, partly because of the way in which we learn to use the term, and because in our language it carries the meaning of "oneness." In actuality, the term represents a complex set of internal states (inside the skin), each of which relates to aspects of the external world outside the skin.

You might like to try the interesting experiment of not saying "I" for an hour at a party or some similar social gathering where you will be talking with many different people.

Each time you start to say "I," stop and reformulate the thought differently. Who or what is it, that is speaking?

Such an exercise may help you discover the various complexities obscured by the sloppy little pronoun "I."

This exercise, and the others suggested in this chapter, may help you to shed your acquired covering of personality, at least temporarily.

A more direct means of doing this utilizes meditation, and in the light of this chapter's discussion, you might like to try meditating again with the aim of uncovering your essence.

Sit quietly for a moment and let your attention roam systematically throughout your body. Be aware of your feet, your ankles, your legs. Is that you? Sense your skin, your ears, your eyes, your stomach, lungs, heart. Are these you? Can you realize that all of these appendages are not you?

Meditate with the following seed thoughts: "I am not my physical body but that which uses it. I am not my emotions but that which controls them, I am not my mental images but that which creates them. I am." Let other thoughts and sensations quietly fade away. Reach for a higher state of consciousness.

Man in his ignorance, identifies himself with the material sheaths that encompass his true Self. Transcending these, he becomes one with Brahman, who is pure bliss.

When all the senses are stilled, when the mind is at rest, when the intellect wavers not—then, say the wise, is reached the highest state.

—*The Upanishads*

We tend to identify with our "material sheaths": the color of our skin, the cut of our face, our sex, or the shape of our bodies. We live through our bodies, but we are not our bodies. The body is a temple in which our true self resides, our personality merely decorates the outer temple. Personality dictates our relation to the external world, whereas our essence connects us to a higher consciousness. As an exercise:

Look into the mirror and be here-now with yourself, with your physical appearance. Do not evaluate. Just be here-now. Do not judge, do not worry, do not compare, just look. Be as impartial as you can. What is the real you? Try the exercise more than once.

If we think of the physical body or the borrowed personality as the whole of us, we will feel threatened when anyone or anything attacks it. We bristle with anger when someone criticizes our behavior, as if our total being were about to be annihilated. If we undergo some form of psychoanalysis or therapy, we may experience anxiety when these acquired traits are questioned, especially if we strongly identify with them. We may fear that there will be nothing underneath.

Some persons feel anxious and threatened when they are deeply loved by another, for love penetrates and temporarily destroys the cloak of personality. In loving, essences seek to unite. This union cannot readily take place if personalities block the flow of energy. On the other hand, if one wishes to develop his essence, love can be one of the strongest forces in our lives. But we cannot totally control this force and it can sometimes cause us painful experiences. As Kahlil Gibran wrote:

> When love beckons to you, follow him,
> Though his ways are hard and steep.
> And when his wings enfold you yield to him,
> Though the sword hidden among his pinions may wound you.
> And when he speaks to you believe in him,
> Though his voice may shatter your dreams as the north wind lays waste the garden.
> For even as love crowns you so shall he crucify you.
> Even as he is for your growth so is he for your pruning. . . .
> And think not you can direct the course of love, for love, if it finds you worthy, directs your course.
>
> —*The Prophet*

If we make the effort, we can begin to shed some of our personality bit by bit, without the trauma of a shattering experience or the expensive operation of psychoanalysis or psychotherapy. Every moment of our daily lives affords some opportunity for observing our mental and physical behavior, and for gently detaching the personality from our inner essence. We must start with simple things, however.

For example, the next time you suffer some minor injury or ailment, perhaps resulting from your own careless inattention

(your failure to be here-now with your body or with what you were doing), try to disidentify. Say to yourself: "My foot hurts, but I do not hurt," or "My head aches, but I do not ache," or "Here is aching," or "My body is tired, but I am not tired." Make the effort to separate your essence from the pain in your material organism.

As you become more in touch with your inner self try this variation of an exercise from Chapter III again:

Focus your attention on the external world. Then on your feeling of essence. Coordinate your breathing with this. As you breathe in, breathe in the world. Collect yourself—try to contact the you that is essence. As you breathe out, let yourself flow into the world.

If you contact your essence-self as you do this exercise you will be filled in a different way with the sensory impressions of the world. It is a good and joyful experience.

One of our most common errors is assuming that negative emotions that well up in us are an integral part of our organism. When you're filled with negative emotions, try to distinguish between "I" and "it." Observe with detachment these emotions that possess you like evil spirits and say, "It is angry at So-and-So again," or "it hates F," or "here is hating," or "it is envious of D." Try not to get caught up in them; they do not originate from essence but have been learned, largely by imitating others. They are passed on from person to person, like diseases. At first, you won't be able to stop their expression very easily, but at least you can avoid the mistake of thinking that they originate within you.

If you become attached to the negative emotions that possess you, you will waste a great deal of energy. On the other hand, if you try to suppress them, you will double the energy loss, since for every action there is an equal and opposite reaction. Ideally, you may be able to direct the energy of negative emotions somewhere less hurtful than at yourself or at others. At least you can recognize that they are not yours.

If you do get caught off guard by emotions of rage, hostility, jealousy, anger, or revenge, go off by yourself and have a full-scale temper tantrum. Scream as loud as you can, hit a couch with your fists, kick a stuffed chair, or lie on your back, kick and pound your fists on a mattress until you have rid yourself of the energy of the emotion. This procedure will bring release to you without harming anyone else. If you can honestly and privately let your negative emotions go, they will have a much weaker hold over your behavior in the future—and they weren't "yours" anyway. Eventually, as you detach from them, negative emotions will come to have a much weaker hold over your behavior, for they are aspects of personality, not essence.

Try also not to identify with your pleasures. When you are engrossed in a very pleasant activity, disidentify from it. Try saying, "My organism is enjoying this ice-cream sundae, but I am not," or "It likes dancing, but I am indifferent," and so forth.

I can almost hear you saying, "But I want to identify with my pleasures! It's right and good to identify with them."

Go ahead and identify with them—but sometime, in an experimental mood, try the exercise. The actual sensation will not change by changing your verbal description of it; only your evaluation of it and your attachment to it may be altered. By means of this exercise, you may distinguish genuine pleasures from those which are only acquired tastes.

Goodness and badness, pleasure and displeasure, are not immutable properties of the outside world; they are simply evaluations made by us. For the most part, our evaluations are only borrowed prejudices and our unconscious and automatic use of them makes it harder for essence to develop. Try to be more detached from your habitual reactions. Let go of your likes and dislikes, your goods and bads, your yes's and no's.

> The Perfect Way knows no difficulties
> except that it refuses all preference.
>
> If you would see the Perfect Way manifest
> Take no thought either for or against it.
> To oppose what you like and what you dislike,
> That is the malady of the mind.
>
> Do not try to find the truth,
> Merely cease to cherish opinions,
> Tarry not in dualism.
>
> As soon as you have good and evil
> Confusion follows and the mind is lost. . . .
>
> When no discrimination is made between this and that
> How can a biased and prejudiced vision arise?
>
> Let-go, leave things as they may be. . . .
>
> Whereas in the Dharma itself there is no individuation
> The ignorant attach themselves to particular objects.
>
> The enlightened have no likes or dislikes.
>
> Gain and loss, right and wrong,
> Away with them once and for all!
>
> The ultimate end of things, beyond which they cannot go
> Is not subject to rules and measures. . . .
>
> It matters not how things are conditioned,
> Whether by "being" or by "not being".
>
> That which is, is the same as that which is not.
> That which is not is the same as that which is. . . .
>
> —Seng-t'san (Third Patriarch of Zen), from "On Believing in Mind"

Do not make the error of thinking that I suggest some kind of Stoic behavior, sitting unflinching and impassive, in the face of joy and sorrow alike. To wall off or suppress natural reactions, emotions, or movements is neither healthy nor desirable. Do not try to block them; try instead to be conscious of them as reactions and to understand to what degree they are acquired and to what degree they are innate. Experience pleasure and suffer pain, but *do not lose your Self* in these emotions. Maintain an altitude of mind; break the association between Self and body. As it is written in *The Upanishads:*

> This body is mortal, always gripped by death, but within it dwells the immortal Self. This Self, when associated in our consciousness with the body, is subject to pleasure and pain; and so long as this association continues, freedom from pleasure and pain no man finds. But as this association ceases, there cease also the pleasure and the pain.

Dropping the cherished cloak of personality is a hard task. Your personality may have been a hindrance and an obstacle, but its operations are at least familiar to you. As you begin to shed it, you may feel very naked indeed. Nearly everything that you formerly considered to be you may have to go. Your friends may find an unpredictable stranger in your place. We live most of our lives in aspects of acquired personality and a great percentage of it in states of negative emotions. People always criticize this or that person, or group, or nation, or complain about themselves endlessly and automatically, like broken records. If you remain silent, rather than let "it" talk, you will find you are left alone with yourself more and more frequently; you may even feel that you are dying; that there is nothing left of you; that life is meaningless and empty. You may have to go through feelings of loneliness, despair, and nothingness before essence can emerge, to be nurtured and developed. In a psychological sense, you must die to be reborn to a more permanent life. Essence constitutes one element of our being that transcends ordinary space and time. We learn to think that time has a beginning and an end to everything, but who is to say this is the truth? Leave the way open to other possibilities. Peek out of your personality into the universe! You can be free—if you choose and if you make the effort.

Do not try to cling to your pleasures. It is as impossible as attempting to catch sunshine in a box. Do not stop your tears. It will not help you to ask why you are sad. Avoid secondary thoughts. All things are transient, your happiness as well as your sorrow, and secondary thoughts will bring you nothing but suffering.

The bamboo shadows are sweeping the stairs,
But no dust is stirred.
The Moonlight penetrates the depths of the pool,
But no trace is left in the water.

—*Zen teaching*

2

BREAKING
THE SHACKLES OF TIME

The boundaries of our conceptions of time are the boundaries of our ordinary consciousness, for time forms the framework within which ordinary consciousness operates. Understanding time provides a key to the freedom of higher consciousness. Alternative ways of viewing time make possible alternative states of consciousness, and as our views of time change so may our consciousness.

Living in the simple here-now connects our inner consciousness to the time-flow observed in the physical world; whereas switching from the simple to the transcendental here-now places us outside of ordinary time.

These are easy words to write or read; understanding them is far more difficult. In this section of the book I deal initially with the formulations of time and space developed by modern physics, and then go on to construct models for the operation of higher consciousness. The first chapter will describe Einstein's theory of relativity; the second will describe a "psychological time" which does not follow ordinary time laws; the third chapter picks up some advanced notions of time from nuclear physics, and in the last chapter a five-dimensional framework of "times" is postulated in which a higher consciousness might operate. The material is more technical and more difficult to read than that of Part 1 and the exercises are fewer and more subtle in their effects. The reader may be inclined to skip over the more technical material, and he may do so without loss of continuity. However, I urge him to try all the exercises at least once in the order presented before reading on.

| VIII |

What Is Time? Is It Now?

Alice sighed wearily. "I think you might do something better with the time," she said, "than wasting it in asking riddles that have no answers."

"If you knew Time as well as I do," said the Hatter, "you wouldn't talk about wasting *it*. It's a *him*."

"I don't know what you mean," said Alice.

"Of course you don't!" the Hatter said, tossing his head contemptuously. "I dare say you never even spoke to Time!"

"Perhaps not," Alice cautiously replied; "but I know I have to beat time when I learn music."

"Ah! That accounts for it," said the Hatter. "He won't stand beating. Now, if you only kept on good terms with him, he'd do almost anything you liked with the clock."

—Lewis Carroll

Seconds, minutes, hours, days, years and eons; the passage of the sun across the sky, the burning of a candle, the moving hands of a clock, the progression of seasons, the decay of an atomic nucleus, and the aging of our bodies; all of these events mark the passage of time. But what *is* time really? Time is measured in many ways, involved in all processes, but what is time itself? Can we point to it? What can we say about it? How can we catch hold of this mysterious, elusive, yet vitally basic aspect of the universe?

Time is the essence of consciousness, or the bane of existence. It is the curse of the impatient, the bored, and the hedonist. Time flies. time kills, time heals all wounds—and yet, time does not exist. There is only duration—the measured interval between two motions or events—the burning of a candle between two marks, the dribbling of sand through an hourglass, the ebb and flow of sea tides, the sparking decay of millions of atomic nuclei, or the steady turning of the earth upon its axis and its spiral motions amongst the stars. There is no time; only events, motions, happenings.

One of the most common notions of time makes it analogous to the flow of a river, endless and inexorable. We humans are caught in its flow—we are born into it, carried along, and die, leaving not a ripple. The river of time flows only one way, neither stopping nor turning back. As Omar Khayyam wrote in "The Rubáiyát":

> The Moving Finger writes; and, having writ,
> Moves on; Nor all your Piety nor Wit
> Shall lure it back to cancel half a Line,
> Nor all your Tears wash out a Word of it.

Prior to 1900 this was the view of time taken by Western culture. Scientists divided the universe into two grand forms: static space and flowing time. They considered space as three dimensional and infinite in all directions and time as one dimensional, irreversible, infinite, and perpetually flowing at a uniform speed. Time and space were separate attributes of the universe, independent and unconnected in any way. The dimension of time was then divided into three parts: past, present, and future.

Einstein's theory of relativity demolished this simplistic notion of a linear, objective "time." His paper, published in 1905, showed that time and space were not uniform but varied depending on the speed of the observer. He reintegrated our view of the universe, reducing the terms "space" and "time" to mere words, not to be taken as real things in themselves, but only as shadowy indications of an underlying wholeness.

Einstein based his theory on the experimental finding that the speed of light is finite and unaffected by any motion of the source of the light. Even though the velocity of light exceeds any other known thing, it still takes a little bit of time for a light ray to travel from one place to another. Therefore, when we use light rays to measure the length of an object a small amount of time passes while the ray travels from the observer to the object being measured. If the object to be measured is also in motion, then it will cover a bit of space during the bit of time that the light ray is in transit. The result will be a change in the *measured length* of the object in the direction of motion, relative to the case in which the object is stationary. If two observers, one moving, one stationary, measure the same object's length, their results will differ.

The relative motion of an observer also affects measured time intervals, for a measurement of time usually requires a comparison between two points in space, as in looking at the moving hand of a clock or meter needle, observing the position of the earth in relation to the sun or the stars, noting the height of a burning candle, etc. If either the observer or the time-process being observed moves, then this motion combines with the speed of the measuring light rays to alter the observed time.

For instance, you may want to compare time intervals with an astronaut on the way to the moon. If he signals "now" when his watch's second hand crosses the twelve mark and "now" when it again reaches the twelve mark, his sixty seconds will be different from yours because there exists a small time delay in the radio transmission of the first "now" and a different small time delay in the radio transmission of his second "now."* The astronaut's sixty seconds will appear to be longer to you than the sixty seconds as measured by your watch.

If an astronaut travels at nine tenths of light velocity, his minute-interval will appear to be nearly two minutes to an earthbound observer. If he travels at the incredibly high speed of 99 per cent that of light, the stationary observer will see his minute as being seven minutes long. But to the astronaut, sixty seconds will still be sixty seconds.

From such simple examples we can readily see that the act of measuring space always includes a time interval and that the act of measuring time always includes a space interval. Time and space are inextricably interrelated. If different observers traveling at different velocities measure the same objective things, their results will differ.

Under such conditions time and space lose their immutability and become plastic variables. For two observers in relative motion, there is no common simultaneous "present." A different "now" exists for each of them. We already know that this is the case with our subjective psychological experience and, with the advent of Einstein's work, we find that it is also true in a strict physical sense.

Not only does time vary with the motion of the observer, it also varies with the strength of the gravitational field. Einstein predicted this in the early 1900s and physicists have experimentally verified this prediction in the last ten years. Such a

*Radio waves, X-rays, ultraviolet and infrared rays all travel at the same velocity as light as far as we can determine, for they are all only names for electromagnetic radiation of different wave lengths.

view may seem to violate our common sense; but that common sense arose from our linguistic conditioning. And, of course, the effect is not noticeable under ordinary conditions of observation.

Korzybski saw that our difficulty in understanding Einstein's seemingly radical views resulted from our objectified language, which directs us automatically to think of a noun as a person, place, or thing, having concrete reality. Korzybski wrote: "The answer to the question, what 'are' the *terms* 'matter,' 'space,' and 'time,' is as usual, given in the properly formulated question. They 'are' terms. . . ."* Nothing more. They are convenient, sometimes useful symbols created by men, not given us by gods from above. If we choose, we can remake them. Einstein chose to do so.

Einstein's work led to two results that have profoundly altered our entire scientific outlook and resulted in radical changes in the philosophy of science: (A) time and space are only aspects of a unified, indivisible whole, and (B) we cannot talk meaningfully about a physical property of the universe without also taking into account a means of measuring it. I will develop these ideas in later chapters.

Fortunately, however, you don't have to understand the developments of modern mathematics and physics to change your way of using words and seeing the world. In Chapter II, I suggested that you can attain the same level of consciousness if you dissolve the screen of words which imprisons and categorizes your perceptions. It is not a matter of learning physics and mathematics, but of freeing yourself, even if only temporarily, from operating by traditional linguistic patterns.

Nevertheless, words have great power over us. We still hang on to the notion that "time" must have some elusive, undefinable essence. We have a vague feeling that time is some "thing" that

*Science and Sanity. Non-aristotelian Publishing Co., 1933 (p. 227).

we can't quite define or lay our hands on, but a real something nevertheless. Although we understand intellectually that "time" is only a term made by a man, we find it hard to feel this solidly and viscerally. Many years of training in the use of our language cannot be undone by a single act of will.

One aid in reducing the power of words over us comes from studying how people of other cultures and other languages deal with time and duration. Natives on the South Pacific island of Truk, for example, do not have a way of expressing the "pastness" of events. For them, then is now. Past events do not disappear or become out of date, but stack up, placing an ever-increasing burden on the Trukese as they try to live and operate in the present. For many years Trukese life was characterized by violent and bloody warfare. Years after some slight had occurred, someone would remember it and arouse his tribe to a fresh attack on the enemy. Isolated villages would be attacked without notice or apparent provocation. One wonders if paranoia was a common symptom among the Trukese.

The Burmese language is tenseless; past, present, and future are not important; the language talks about actions regardless of the time they take place in. Past and future find their reality only in the present. Verbs stand for immediately known actions. That is why most Burmese are not happy if they have to make scheduled appointments. For them time is relative and subjective —the time it takes for a pot of rice to cool, or the time the sun sets, changing with the seasons and with human intention. For the Burmese, time is indeed a plastic variable.

While for our culture Einstein used complicated mathematics to show that time was not an absolute, the Hopi Indians of Arizona have never needed either the word or the concept. According to Benjamin Lee Whorf, a linguist who studied their language, the Hopi have no terms for past, present, and future. Instead they have terms that can be roughly translated as "manifest" or "objective," and "unmanifest" or "subjective."

The objective or manifest comprises all things and events that are or have been accessible to the senses; thus it includes the past and the present. Sunsets, trees, other people's bodies, rocks, and ashtrays are all termed manifest or objective if they have been or are external events, impinging on our senses.

The subjective or unmanifest refers to all that appears and exists in the mind, or as the Hopi would say, "in the heart." The real future then, is only a portion of the subjective realm. The unmanifest realm also includes hopes, desires, wishes, and any other kinds of "if" trips. As the unmanifest becomes the manifest, we might say that the imaginary becomes real. The Hopi notion of the unmanifest includes not just what is in the mind of man but also what is in the inner heart or core of animals, plants, things—in fact, in the heart of the universe itself. For instance, in the actual growth of corn, the formation of clouds and their condensation into rain, in the planning and carrying out of communal activities, the Hopis perceive the unmanifest becoming manifest.

Whatever is hoped for, wished for, or strived for, is deemed unmanifest and in the subjective, mental realm. It does *not,* however, advance toward manifestation out of a distant future; it is *already present* in vital form. Whether or not something unmanifest becomes manifest is a different matter. Things may change from the unmanifest to the manifest or they may not, but the Hopi's here-now incorporates both realms. As subjective events become more definite and more assured, they become more manifest. But they do not change in a serial fashion—one by one, minute by minute, day by day—rather, events flow, merge, and overlap, growing into manifestation, much as plants grow. The Hopi is assured of his wife's making a blanket in two more days, although the finished blanket is not entirely manifest yet.

The manifest or objective merely involves a coming to fruition of the inner thoughts, desires, or purposes of everything in the world. Every living and nonliving thing has its private core of unmanifest desires; what becomes manifest, what becomes public and real, arises from some average of the covert desires of everything and everyone.

Once something has become manifest it does not disappear into the past. To the Hopi, it is implicit that everything that ever happened still is. The here-now of the Hopi includes what we call the past and what we call the future as well as what we call the imaginary. It might be much easier for Hopis to experience the transcendental here-now described in Chapter IV because of their cultural-linguistic background than it is for us.

Based upon his study of the Hopi language, Whorf astutely picked out some other awkward ways in which we think about time. He said that our objectified, spatialized view of time dulls our sense of the cumulative value of innumerable small moments. He writes:

> To us, for whom time is motion on a space, unvarying repetition seems to scatter its force along a row of units of that space, and be wasted. To the Hopi, for whom time is not a motion, but a "getting later" of everything that has ever been done, unvarying repetition is not wasted but accumulated. It is a storing up of an invisible change that holds over into later events.*

Every teacher knows the difficulty of getting pupils to recognize that repetitive practice is not a "waste of time," but only hindsight enables us to sing out to others that "practice makes perfect."

In our language we split time into discrete parts just as if it

* *Language, Thought, and Reality*, p. 151.

were a material thing, like sand or water. We talk about chunks of time. We speak of "a moment" of time and unconsciously think of time as a succession of separate, distinct moments. This makes it harder for us to visualize the whole of events and their organic development from tiny seeds into full bloom. It probably makes it harder for us to plan ahead—we are always "fighting against time" or striving to "make more time." We not only still consider time an objective thing, Einstein notwithstanding, but we think it an enemy, an evil thing thwarting our every desire!

Our notions of the objectlike structure of time have led us to keeping records, diaries, accounting journals, time graphs, and related symbolic devices. We talk about "saving" time, as if it were so many units of things to be hoarded and spent. Such an emphasis upon time leads us to a high evaluation of speed, which shows up in much of our behavior. We are always hurrying into the next moment, but the next moment, like tomorrow's jam, never comes. By hurrying into the future we easily miss the present, which means we easily miss living fully. "I haven't got time," we say and hurry away like the white rabbit. If we are forever making time to save time, we'll never have time to spend time. Time cannot be made, saved, had, or spent. It is always, only now.

In my opinion the Hopi view of time falls more in accordance with the operation of our consciousness. Our ordinary view of time is simply a habit of thought. This habit developed in us along with our speech patterns at about the age of three. We learned words for time and naturally absorbed rules of their use. We were taught about yesterday, promised candy tomorrow, fed at dinnertime, bedded at naptime and generally integrated into Western society according to notions of linear, serialized time. Yet the physical world is certainly not divided into a past, present, and future. Somebody made up those concepts and now each succeeding generation tries to force the world to fit them.

Modern physics has discarded them, and the Hopis never acquired them. This attachment to linear time as a one-dimensional "thing" that flows from the past to the future unnecessarily limits the free flow of our consciousness. While we don't have to study Hopi language or modern physics, doing so may aid the reopening of our consciousness.

We usually ignore science and relegate its study to a few specialists, but if we look closely we see that it affects our entire world outlook; it is more significant than something to help us make better gadgets, faster automobiles, or antibiotics and tranquilizers. Einstein's work profoundly altered our views of time and of physical reality as something "absolute"; and he thereby not only helped make the atomic bomb possible, but also paved the way for a change in our consciousness, which is intimately bound up with how we perceive time and the world.

His work, in conjunction with the study of the Hopi language, provides a basis for a new conception of time and of reality which I shall discuss in the next few chapters.

> Time is a word that we have formerly believed to be a thing.
>
> —Adapted from HENRI POINCARÉ

Psychological Time

"I don't understand you," said Alice. "Its dreadfully
confusing!"

"That's the effect of living backwards," the Queen said
kindly: "it always makes one a little giddy at first————"

"Living backwards!" Alice repeated in great astonishment.
"I never heard of such a thing!"

"—but there's one great advantage in it, that one's
memory works both ways."

"I'm sure *mine* only works one way," Alice remarked. "I
can't remember things before they happen." "It is a poor
sort of memory that only works backwards," the Queen
remarked.

—LEWIS CARROLL

"A tree stark and black against the reddening sky."

"Sitting on a rock immersed in the sound and sight of dancing
blue-white foam."

"Eating an apple on the back porch in the warm October
afternoon sun."

"The face of my darling, smiling at me from across the
room."

Memories of things past which never lose their sparkle. Memories of another, long ago time more vivid and real than all of yesterday's, or last month's or last year's. "Memories that linger, constant and true" while most everyday activities blend together and dissolve as time passes, leaving only fragments that say they ever were.

We all know this "queerness" of inner experience, but actually, it's not queer at all—it's merely what happens. Perhaps it only seems odd because we base our ideas of what memory should be on our classical conceptions about the nature of time.

Thoughts, memories, and inner experience do not seem to follow the man-made model of physical time. They are not always arranged in linear fashion, but follow their own psychological arrangements. Moreover, they also come invested with an extra dimension of depth or intensity. Vivid and exciting memories pop into one's head more often than prosaic ones.

Unpleasant memories, on the other hand, may whirl continuously before the mind's eye, blotting out the past and darkening the present. One can deliberately push such memories away; but they may sneak back now and then to usurp one's attention and drain one's emotional energy. Our remembered lives consist of peculiar hodgepodges of experiences, distorted, blurred, and rearranged by the rules of our psychological make-up, and our sense of past time follows a similar pattern.

In order to talk meaningfully about *human* experience we need to construct a different notion of time than the one used for talking about physical phenomena. We need not adhere to the classical idea of linear, constant time, since Einstein has shattered its foundations and the Hopis provide living evidence of its arbitrariness. Let's call the older notion "clock time" or "physical time" and my new notion "psychological time" or "experiential time." You may find these notions confusing and may wish to formulate your own ideas rather than ingest mine. I don't claim any monopoly on the truth, but, in any case, the exercises and experiments will provide you with experience in reformulating your own thinking and feeling about the world and how you operate in it.

Before turning to the experimental material let's look at time on the neural and physiological levels. In the brain, every sensation consists of a pattern of energy changes that strike a receptor. Sound waves are patterns of energy change propagated in the air. Light waves are alternations of space-time called photons that strike the eyes and induce chemical changes which in turn trigger nerve impulses. The brain acts as the central storehouse for all neural impulses from all the receptors. Different things or events produce different patterns of neural impulses. These are all that the brain has to work with. No elusive, mysterious "essence of time" will be found in your brain or in mine, only hundreds of thousands of neural patterns.

As we live, we compare incoming neural patterns with stored ones, we formulate new arrangements of neural patterns, we scan stored patterns rapidly, and we emit via speech, gestures, writing, or behavior, transformations of the patterns which channel through our brains. When we scan a neural pattern, what tells us whether it is the memory of an event, some anticipated future event, or a here-now happening? Somehow the brain must have a way of discriminating between neural impulses or "events" that occur via the senses and those generated internally. We know, like the Hopi, when something is manifest or objective and when it is unmanifest or subjective. When this neural discriminator breaks down, we have hallucinations or perhaps even psychosis.

Although the ability to discriminate between the objective and the subjective may be innate, learning, culture, and our linguistic heritage clearly modify our discrimination. The verbalized attitudes of others become our own internal rules for shuffling and categorizing the neural impulses in the brain, differentiating between the real and the surreal, and forming our sense of time. Through consensual validation obtained by communication with others we learn which neural patterns to accept as manifest and which to reject as unmanifest or surreal.

As sensations flicker through the brain they are codified and stored. There is evidence that the brain records every detail of our experience. People under hypnosis, or people whose brains were directly stimulated by weak electric currents have recalled previous experiences in minute detail—sometimes more detail than they can consciously recall. And even if the brain does not record every experience, it contains enough storage capacity to do so.

It is my hypothesis that the brain employs two separate recording systems: one for all impressions that enter it, and another one for impressions to which we consciously attend. The first one operates in a straightforward manner, mechanically recording our experiences and sensations. It stores information in linear clock time, limited only by the coarseness of our sensory receptors and the information-handling capacity of our nervous systems. We have practically no access with our conscious mind to most of the material in this memory bank, although it may be accessible to our higher consciousness or the higher consciousness of others.*

The second system records only those important or exciting events which we consciously attend to. It is laid out within a nonlinear, multidimensional framework and may be neurologically quite different from the first one. I don't know what actually

*A woman with psychic abilities once looked at me and said: "I see a small boy with an old-fashioned fireman's hat on, sitting in a garden. Would that be your little boy?" Momentarily puzzled I said, "No." But when I thought about the possibilities, I realized that it very likely might have been me thirty years ago since my father was a fireman. Speaking with my father later supported the possibility since he indeed had such a hat once, but he did not remember a specific instance. Since the woman had no knowledge about me directly, perhaps her higher conscious mind picked the scene up from my stored memories.

happens within my brain, but I am aware that when I consciously attend to events, when I am as fully present as I can be with what is happening, it seems as if impressions flow to a different place within me. Perhaps you noticed something like this yourself when you were doing some of the exercises in Chapters III and IV. Daly King* points out that more than half of our sensory impressions seem to dead end in that part of the brain called the cerebellum. He says this noncontinuation of the impulses puzzles neurologists and he suggests that conscious attention to sensory impressions will result in greater use of them by the brain. Professor H. W. Magoun,† suggests that there may be a neural switch in the cerebellum directing excitation into one of two pathways to the muscles. Perhaps there are other neural switching functions as well. You can try the exercises and decide about the effects, if any, for yourself. But first, let's return for a brief look at other ways our organism marks time.

It is well known that the body has its own highly accurate biological clock. Most people can set a mental alarm clock before going to sleep to awaken them at any reasonable hour. I can also set my mental alarm clock to awaken me more fully at a preset time during the day if I wish. Physiologists have not yet discovered how people can internally measure time so accurately. Most of the known body processes that are cyclic such as brain waves, heartbeats, digestive processes, or respiration do not follow clock time accurately enough to account for the precision of our mental alarm clock, although they may be related to our psychological time.

Alpha brain waves, for instance, may function as a scanning frequency for perception. The period of a ten-cycle alpha wave, one tenth of a second, approximates the average minimum time unit for perception. That is, we take in information in bits of time

* *The States of Human Consciousness.* University Books, 1963.
† *The Waking Brain.* Charles C. Thomas, 1958.

which average about ten per second. This denotes the quantum of sensory perception. Psychological time may somehow be related to this unit of time, for some persons report that subjective time rate seems to lengthen while they are in the alpha state. That is, when one is producing alpha waves, more psychological time elapses during the same interval of clock time than is the case when one is engaged in ordinary activities and presumably producing beta waves.

The higher frequency brain waves called beta have been associated with states of anxiety in some subjects. If psychological time varies with brain-wave frequency we might expect that persons in the beta state would perceive clock time as passing more quickly than normal. This ties in well with the common observation that anxious people usually aren't very here-now. They worry about the future or get hung up in the past; time seems rushed to them; they feel harried and hassled.

If indeed brain-wave frequency constitutes a rough measure of psychological time we would expect that lowering the alpha frequency, or coming into theta, would slow down time even more. Perhaps brain waves markedly decrease in frequency during those rare moments of "timelessness," that we sometimes experience. Here is an area for further research.

The heart rate may also interrelate to psychological time, for when we are excited clock time seems to pass more quickly. When we are relaxed, our heart rate usually decreases and clock time seems to slow down. Of course, it is not clock time that varies—that remains constant; rather, psychological time decreases when we are aroused and lengthens when we are relaxed. This relationship is not always consistent, however, for it also is affected by our mental state. If we are relaxed in body and alert in mind, psychological time may increase, but if we are relaxed and bored or dozing, psychological time may fall to a minimum, for we are consciously absorbing only a few of the total available impressions.

In earlier exercises I suggested that the breathing cycle could delimit a natural time unit related to consciously taking in impressions. I have observed that if I attend to my breathing as I attend to the world around me my perceptions seem clearer and more intense, I can more easily be "awake" and psychological time seems fuller. Furthermore, after a few breath cycles, respiration usually slows and deepens. This in turn slows my heart rate and is a precursor to producing alpha rhythms. The relationship between psychological time and physiological cycles is an unexplored one—see what you can discover as you do the exercises. Here is the first one to help you heighten the contrast between psychological and clock time.

Obtain a metronome or loudly ticking clock. Concentrate your attention on the intervals between the ticks. Subjectively try to make them grow longer. Pay attention to all the sensations that you can perceive between the ticks. Keep stretching your awareness to take in more and more sensations between each tick of the clock. Can you begin to get a sense of how much goes on between just two ticks of a clock?

Practice the exercise a few times. Remember to attend to as many internal sensations as you can: your muscle tensions, stomach sensations, posture, tactile awareness, and so on.

As another experiment in differentiating between psychological and clock time try the following:

For ten minutes of clock time do nothing. Do not let your mind wander on purpose, but do not necessarily try to be here-now. Just fix your mind to the purpose of doing nothing for that period. Can you shrink psychological time to zero?

Practically everyone knows the experience of a "psychological time" which runs a different course from clock time. We've all been involved so intensely in situations that the hours seemed like minutes. And I suppose you've also had those periods of intense excitement which seemed like hours in retrospect, though the clock hands had scarcely moved.*

However, because the notion of a linear clock time has been so successful in our science and technology and because there exists no suitable expression for psychological time in our language, we have come to take clock time as the only basis of our lives. Our sense of psychological time has been bludgeoned into the coarse meter of clock time through our upbringing and our acquired language. We acquired our views about time in the same manner as we absorbed other beliefs and attitudes concerning such things as nationalism, race, sex roles, food preferences, political ideologies, or the buying of soap. But the prejudice of time is so subtle and so pervasive that we usually overlook it.

We learn to associate happenings and internal subjective experience with our external awareness of calendars and clocks. We learn when it is time to eat, to sleep, to yell, to have ice cream, to get married, or to work—regardless of how we think or feel. We are rewarded and punished in terms of "tomorrow," "next week," "next summer," or "later." We gradually grow up to see the world through the screen of man-made time and to fit the richness of our own thoughts, feelings, sensations, and loves into the square mesh of seconds, minutes, days, and years.

Language habits determine our views of time as much or more than anything else. In Chapter VIII, I described how we parcel time into pieces like portions of pie and equate each piece with

*Bernard Aaronson, head of the Experimental psychology section at the Bureau of Research in Neurology and Psychiatry in Princeton, New Jersey, has done some fascinating work on time perception using hypnosis. He found that people hypnotized to the notion that there is no past and future, only the here and now, became very relaxed and sociable. But when it was suggested to them that there is no present, one person became catatoniclike in his behavior, locked out of the present, unable to move.

so much money. Besides this, the very way we use symbols constrains us to serialize thoughts, memories, and experiences along a single linear dimension.

We learn to write sentences one word at a time, from left to right across the page; but who thinks that way? Our thoughts crowd into the front of our minds, clamoring for expression all at once. We stutter and stammer and sometimes come to a complete stop from the frustration of trying to speak or write only one word or idea at a time. Squeezing thoughts into sequential form drags down the free-flowing, supralogical thought-process. Our thoughts flow along simultaneous paths like current flowing through parallel elements in an electric circuit. We leap ahead to a conclusion, jump to a supportive statement, sense an implication, run it down quicker than a wink, charge back to challenge a premise, or toss out a hypothesis, and all the while we can write or type only one measly line in slow motion across the paper. Thought is half-murdered in the writing.

As we grow up and learn the rules of language and of logic we simultaneously learn to order things and events in clock time. Our thinking is gradually forced into narrower and narrower channels until we can only write or think in linear time sequences. I believe this hampers our creative ability and limits the expression of our emotions. Just the same, some artists and art forms succeed in breaking through time limitations—Picasso sets a notable example with his simultaneous "time fragments" of one scene or face or object.

In the verbal realm, poets fare better. Their more highly organized allusive use of language does not need to run between the fences of linear logic and serialized, rationalized thinking. There is less loss of emotional expression in poetry too.

Some ordering and selecting is necessary though, even for poets. Such squeezing, filtering, and codifying makes our thoughts communicable to others—at least as we now communicate.

Some people have never learned to force their thoughts into deliberate serial form—their speech consists of stutters, stops, and starts, combined and run-together ideas branching like trees at every comma, making it almost unintelligible. In between chaos and newspaper writing, however, lie some interesting styles of writing and communicating.

To limber up unused thought patterns try the following amusing experiment a few times:

Write or talk (preferably into a tape recorder or to friends). Utter meaningless nonsence, non grammatical, non seqentshal: not all engis not good feeling free: associations: wheels wheezes schuffles skunks bitin sunheatingroaring twisten me free! Gagh . . . poop.

Because most of us learn to order our spoken and written thoughts neatly and tidily in linear form, word by word, idea by idea, one after the other, we assume that inner experience follows the same linear sequence. We have been subtly but strongly induced to force our psychological experience into the kind of ordered sequence that we use for language or that we take to be the basis of physical time.

Such common admonitions as "Live your life one day at a time" or "Worry about today and tomorrow will take care of itself" serve to reinforce a serial notion of time. But psychological time does not operate in that way—it is more fluid, flowing, and free. We've all experienced inner time jumping from event to event, skipping years of clock time in a flash, bringing moments from childhood into our "now," causing past experiences to overshadow the present like thundershowers in March.

Occasionally our sense of time dissolves completely. When we are intensely here-now with some person or some event, or have successfully contacted a higher consciousness through meditation or some other means, we may experience a state of "timelessness"—a tranquil, eternal "now." Such a state is a common denominator of most mystical experiences.

This exercise can help you induce such a state whenever you choose:

> Stop reading for a minute or two and try to be here-now. Quiet your breathing and increase the pauses before and after exhalation. Take in as much of what is going on as you can—the sounds, the motions of things, the flow of feelings within you, the positions and tensions of your body, your thoughts. Especially attend to any other persons, and your own sense of yourself as being present, right here, right now. As you do this, *stop time.* Be aware that everything happening or existing is just as it should be, was to be, will be, is. There is no time, there is only now, this moment.

After you've become familiar with this procedure you might like to try an extension of it with a group. Some of my most beautiful and quietly exciting experiences of such a state have come about as a result of the next exercise. This procedure for helping each other pass into the transcendental here-now was developed by my students at Goddard College in Vermont many years ago, and it is one of the finest I know!

> Gather together a few friends who are familiar with the notion of being here-now and have practiced a bit. Pick a relaxed and pleasant spot away from distractions of noise or other persons and sit closely together so that you can easily see and touch each other. Take a few minutes to attend to what is present—the sensory environment, your own internal states and the presence of those around you. Then concentrate your attention primarily on being with each other. Talk or not as you wish. But help one another not to stray into reveries or away from the group. Try to be fully here-now with each other. Maintain eye contact by looking into the eyes of the others and as you look, feel, and

sense what is going on, *reflect on the timelessness of it. Make the effort to stop time.* Be aware, understand that *there is no time within you,* that here the past and the future flow together into the now and now is forever. This moment is eternal.

I venture that you won't forget the results of this experience too soon. After all, since time is man's invention it is also his plaything. It is not so hard to think like a Hopi Indian or an Einstein once we open the door.

I like to think of clock time as the beat, and psychological time as the melody of our experience. In any given period of clock time each individual has his own melody of sensory impressions. Our inner lives are symphonies played against the steady beat of physical time.

The richness of psychological time depends on whether or not we are bored or interested in our environment. Each moment of clock time contains as many events and impressions as we can comfortably attend to; and the recollection of these events marks the passage of our psychological time. For example, when we recall the day, what is it that we recall? It is not the steady ticks of the clock or the number of swings of the pendulum. It is events—things that happen to us, circumstances through which we pass—ongoing processes which make their big or little impressions in our brain. Not "time" but happenings give us our sense of duration and existence.

During a day, the first event may be struggling to get up, followed by eating breakfast, then going to work, meeting with someone, writing a report, making phone calls, eating lunch, and-so on. While eating lunch we may be reviewing our report, or discussing our morning meeting, or thinking about what we will be doing that afternoon. While we are making phone calls we may also be planning our work schedule; while we are going home we may be reviewing business plans.

The events of the day overlap and interact; when one event

begins and another ends partly depends on what we attend to, what attracts us, and what happens in the world around us. But seldom does inner time follow the same orderly progression that clock time steadily marks.

For example, you say that the clock reads 11:30, but what is going on? What happenings are you in? Time is not 11:30—what would that mean to a Hopi Indian or a Pigmy of the Phillipine Islands? The degree of your consciousness of events around you delineates time, not the position of hands on a clock face. Happenings, not clocks, involve us and give us a sense of living and a sense of the passage of time. The more events involve us, or rather, the more we involve ourselves in them, the fuller and richer our psychological time becomes. Sometimes, though, we can get attached to events by our negative emotions and psychological time comes to a temporary stop.

If I have trouble starting my car and I am late to work, I become irritated and remain locked in by that event all morning. That one small incident can infect every aspect of my behavior. I observe myself growling at the slowpoke driver in front of me, I make stupid errors like missing my exit, compounding my lateness and increasing my bad mood. I fail utterly to notice the beauty of the clear day around me. Instead I find myself thinking that none of these things would have happened if I had the money for a good car, that I would have the money if it weren't for such and such a reason, etc. I whirl the whole affair around in my head, nursing my irritation and needlessly justifying myself, blowing my irritation on those around me like disease germs, hoping that I can sucker other people into identifying with me. In a mild, but destructive way I develop a hang-up that prevents me from being here-now.

Suppose someone slights me and I feel hurt? I may be caught up by my negative interpretations of that event for a long while, my energy and attention absorbed in self-pitying and vengeful fantasies. Have you ever known anyone who nursed a grudge for years and years? How long could you make the sting of a trivial rejection last if you really wanted to? What kind of accounts do you keep against others? How many of your hang-ups are self-imposed? Why do you hang on to them?

If I don't choose what I attend to, then the past can control me, for it captures my inner attention; but if I do choose, then I can influence not only my psychological past but my psychological future as well.

As long as I am continually choosing and discarding I am free. I can be fully with another person or with whatever is going on. But negative feelings or memories of past hurts can color my present outlook and affect my future life. Though there is an objective past and my body may bear its scars, my memories comprise the only past I really know. In this sense the psychological past still lives alongside the psychological present. If I suffered some injury in a car accident years ago I may fear cars to this day. My memories of the past affects my present behavior. If I change the focus of my inner attention, re-evaluate those memories, and release the feelings attached to them I will affect the present and the future as well.

After all, what is memory but the distillation of your psychological time? If you think back on your life you will see how memory works on a large scale. For instance, think of moments when you were most conscious, most here-now, most excited, and interested in what you were doing. That glorious summer in Europe, that vacation in Florida, that month you spent with So-and-So, etc. Or perhaps moments of intense quiet when you were in touch with your inner self or in communication with nature. How often and how deeply have such events entered into your life? Do they still remain with you in an active way? In fact, what else is your life? If you review your life you will see that the most important, the most personal, the fullest and richest parts of it are nothing other than your memories of salient events. What do you retain from early childhood, from high-school days, or from college years? Perhaps you retain only the few big moments, only a few intense events which linger, interspersed with countless meaningless fragments, random glimpses of happenings, like snapshots.

In contrast to these periods of excitement, reflect on intervals when you were uninterested in what you were doing, when you held a dull job, or lived in a dull place—or perhaps yesterday afternoon, when you were tired and bored with your work. When you think back on such times, you may find that you have no memories of them, or that your recollections are practically out of reach. You only know that such periods existed because of external records, of the passage of clock time, and the aging of your body. You might as well have been asleep; certainly your awareness of events was asleep. Clock time runs steadily, but psychological time varies with the degree of our consciousness.

When we are busy and alert, psychological time expands and clock time seems to pass quickly. But in retrospect our memories swarm with images and sensations. When we are bored, clock time seems to pass slowly; we do not attend to our environment and we do not remember it; psychological time and memory shrink practically to zero.

We create our psychological time and determine the quality of our lives by our conscious efforts. Because only those events to which we attend leave any permanent impression on us, we generally lead lives that are less full than they might be. Often only strongly negative or highly positive events succeed in awakening our consciousness. Knowing this, some individuals seek out events to stimulate and force them into being here-now, that is, into being conscious. Drugs, car races, sky diving, mountain climbing, and excitement of all sorts produce strong impressions which force consciousness to increase and psychological time to expand.* Violent passions or even severe sickness and mental illness can sometimes put people in states of heightened consciousness, for the acquired personality temporarily fades out in such conditions. People often engage in strange antics just to obtain experiences that will make them really feel alive. Even a painful experience seems better than none at all.

By making a conscious effort to take in impressions, however, we can charge each moment as fully as the most exciting ones. We can fill up our lives, our consciousness, and our psychological time and as we do so, our life will become steadier and more meaningful. We can expand our psychological time tenfold if we make just a little effort.

Every moment abounds with exhilarating impressions. It is merely a matter of training one's self to actively notice the plenum of impressions and happenings, switching them into your consciousness instead of passively allowing them to calcify in your mechanical memory.

For instance, you may begin by attending to little things and events which you ordinarily ignore. In Chapters II and III I discussed expanding your sensory awareness and increasing your ability to be present, or here-now, to what's happening. Continue the same line of work, keeping in mind the desire to take in impressions within the framework of psychological time rather than clock time.

Events and happenings often have several parallel lines of

*Marijuana seems to increase the awareness of impressions thereby increasing psychological time and affecting the perceived time rate. When "high," people report that time seems to slow down, since for a given clock time they take in more impressions. Unfortunately, however, the drug may take energy from other functions of the organism and usually reduces the control which the person has over his emotions, or over which impressions he attends to. People often report that they feel logy and enervated the day after being high.

development. Ordinarily, we attend only to one ongoing event (or at least we are told that we should operate in that fashion), but if we open up our attention and work at developing that muscle called the brain, we will quickly see that a different way of living, thinking, and perceiving becomes possible.

Although we never seem to have enough clock time (which is, after all, finite), we can expand our psychological time indefinitely. Since we cannot crowd more events into our culturally given form of clock time, we must learn to perceive happenings as simultaneous which we now perceive only one at a time, or perhaps not at all. It may sound paradoxical at first, but give it a try.

> **Write down what you are immediately aware of. Begin each sentence with: "Now I am aware of . . ." or "here is . . ." As you write, observe your pen moving, the letters forming, the muscles in your arm tensing and relaxing; simultaneously attend to what you are hearing, feeling, thinking, or doing with some other part of your body.**

You may notice that it doesn't take any more real clock time to register the different sensations, only a little more effort. For myself, I find that if I closely attend to my writing, to the letters forming, the pen moving, etc., this close attention actually clarifies and enhances the other sensations that are present. Furthermore, I can try this exercise with whatever I am doing. I just have to remember to make the effort, since I've been habituated to one-track thinking for so many years.

Each minute we receive hundreds of sense impressions, perform dozens of movements, and are subject to hundreds of inner sensations such as muscular contractions, breathing, changes of temperature, aspects of digestion or hunger, and so on. If we choose, we can become conscious of many of these impressions for they are all neurologically present in the brain.

We usually have so little consciousness of the marvelous life of our body that we might as well have no body at all. Except on special occasions, when our body calls our attention to itself, we treat it as a mere machine.

We are sometimes as unaware of our emotional life as we are of our physical bodies. We think we govern our emotions but detached observation of our feelings will soon convince us that they seem to be independent of our volition and desires.

The same applies to our intellectual life, as you may have discovered if you meditated along the lines suggested in Chapter V. Thoughts come and go; we can command neither their presence nor their absence in our consciousness under ordinary conditions, although with the advent of brain-wave training we may effect some changes.

Some people may attend to more of their emotional life than others, and certain specialists may be aware of their physical bodies to a greater degree than others; but how many persons are simultaneously aware of, say, their emotions and their physical organism? Generally, we attend to more than one aspect only when some intense external event excites us at two or more levels. What and how much we attend to depends more on change than our conscious will.

The following exercises may help you increase your simultaneous awareness of your environment:

A. Take a notebook and write down as many external events as you can that you are presently involved in. For example, you may be writing this exercise. You are also existing in a room, some specific place in the world. You are perhaps going to school this year or employed as a builder. You are working on a certain project for yourself. You are on a committee, etc.

B. Write down as many feelings as you can be aware of right now. Even if you are not aware of any feelings, take your pencil

and start writing. Make up a few feelings to prime your awareness and others will probably come bubbling up. Try this exercise every day for a while.

C. Get up and walk around, concentrate your attention on your physical body. Plan some definite action in your head: something very simple such as getting up, walking across the room, and sitting down in another chair. Plan it in the greatest possible detail. Think and visualize how you will move toward the chair, how and which way you will turn around and lower yourself. What you will do with your hands when you sit down. How you will hold your head as you sit down. Then do it. What happens?

D. Try to combine awareness of your feelings with awareness of your physical movements. Set aside a certain definite and small amount of clock time for trying this, say one minute. (Don't give up after one attempt, though.)

If you persist in these exercises you will triple your psychological time. This method is not introspective or psychoanalytic. You are required only to be aware. To expand your consciousness is to expand your life, your time, and your energy. Here and now is a very big place.

> The minutes have got to be mine,
> For if the minutes are not mine,
> The days go by, and they are not mine,
> And the years go by, lost forever.

—BRUCE BRITTON

| X |

Transcending Space-Time

Alice was just beginning to say "There's a mistake somewhere———," when the Queen began screaming, so loud that she had to leave the sentence unfinished. "Oh, oh, oh!" shouted the Queen, shaking her hand about as if she wanted to shake it off. "My finger's bleeding! Oh, oh, oh, oh!"

Her screams were so exactly like the whistle of a steam-engine, that Alice had to hold both her hands over her ears.

"What *is* the matter?" she said, as soon as there was a chance of making herself heard. "Have you pricked your finger?"

"I haven't pricked it *yet*," the Queen said, "but I soon shall———oh, oh, oh!"

—Lewis Carroll

We have mistakenly been led to believe that time and space form the boundaries of our world, but experiences of higher consciousness, however momentary, contradict this. We all have flashes of extraordinary consciousness at times, and though they may be accidental and transitory, they are real to us. We generally cannot force them to happen, but by moderate efforts,

132

coupled with understanding, we may increase the frequency of their occurrence.

In this and the following chapter I shall enlarge your understanding of psychological time and higher consciousness by drawing upon more ideas from physics. Symbolic mastery of any skill often precedes actual mastery. We learn many things intellectually before we understand them at gut level. If we learn about the ways in which physicists have *symbolically* transcended the limitations of space-time, it may help pave the way toward our direct experience of such a state of consciousness.

As you may recall from the discussion in Chapter VIII, Einstein found that the finite speed of light forced us to recognize that there were no such things as absolute time and separate, constant space. Both are merely aspects of a whole and must be treated together. He formulated his ideas with the aid of a geometry of four dimensions developed by Hermann Minkowski, a Polish mathematician. Quite simple in notation, although powerful in implication, this geometry will be briefly described in the following pages.

The major idea consists of treating time as a dimension just as we usually treat space. Figure 8 illustrates a simple Minkowski diagram with only one space dimension drawn in for the sake of simplicity.

The lines represent the path of a car. First the car sits in Boston without moving in space, while time goes on. Then it is driven to New York. While being driven, it moves both in time and in space. Then it sits in New York at one point in space while time again passes. Such a diagram is called a "world line" in Minkowski geometry. You can easily imagine the diagram extended indefinitely, with many zigs and zags representing the total world line of a car from its manufacture to its ultimate destruction in some junk yard.

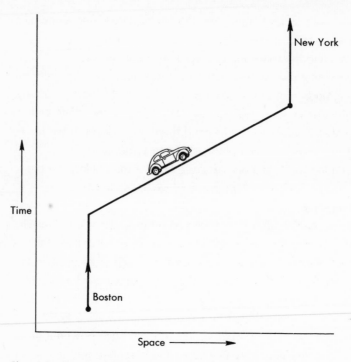

Figure 8. Car traveling from New York to Boston.

One restriction on the diagram is that there can be no absolutely horizontal lines. That would imply an infinite velocity, meaning a car could get from one space point to another in zero time.

This restriction comes from Einstein's formulations and the experimental evidence which led to them: namely that the speed of light is finite and always the same, and that no physical body can exceed the speed of light. Another restriction, that lines must always move upward on the diagram arises from the notion that things must go forward in time. Though the car can move from Boston to New York and back, the path of travel would be as in Figure 9, not as in Figure 10.

The one-wayness of time seems to distinguish it from space dimensions. No one-wayness exists in space; we can apparently move to any place and move back as often as we wish, but we cannot move to and fro in the time direction.

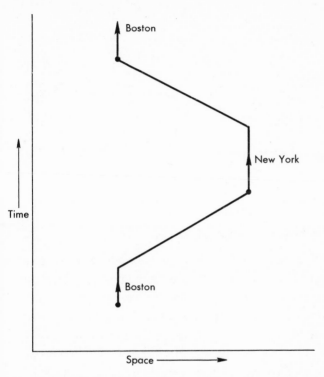

Figure 9. Correct world line of car traveling to New York and back.

Why is time one-way while space is not? Is there something special about the universe that forces time to flow one-way or do we only see it that way? It is true that our memories usually give us the sense of a time-flow in one direction, but as suggested in the previous chapter, these memories and our related notion of time are relative to our culture, our language, and our training.

135   *Transcending Space-Time*

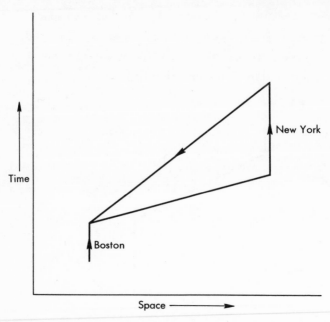

Figure 10. Incorrect world line of car's path.

Besides, one-wayness of time-flow need not be a property of *all* objects and processes in the universe. Some processes indicate a preferred or more probable direction of time: fruit ripens and decays, mountains erode and wash away slowly but surely into the sea, we are born and die, things become mixed up easily but unmixed only with difficulty, etc. Processes of aging and decay are obvious in the case of living things, and happen as well in many realms of the nonliving.

In some areas of modern physics, though, the one-wayness of time has been questioned. In 1949 the physicist Dr. Richard P. Feynman showed that certain phenomena could be described by postulating a backward flow of time. We can explain his basic idea quite easily in terms of the Minkowski four-dimensional diagrams.

Figure 11 shows an electron (e−) and a positron (e+) (or

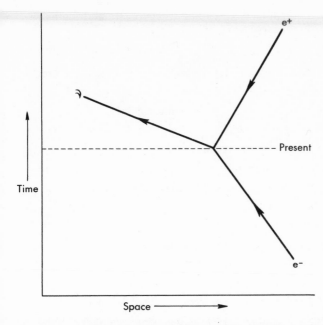

Figure 11. An electron and a positron coming together and changing into a photon.

electron with a positive charge) moving toward each other and meeting at a point. When they meet they annihilate each other, giving off light energy in the form of a bundle of radiation called a photon.

Feynman showed that this interaction between an electron and a positron could be explained by assuming that there was only one particle present, an electron, and that when the photon was given off, the electron began to travel backward in time. He interpreted this change in electric charge from negative to positive as equivalent to a change in direction of the electron's movement through or in time. In other words, positrons are only electrons traveling backward in time.

Such a notion did not violate any basic laws of nature or

known experimental facts according to Feynman, and therefore could be used to make predictions in spite of its strangeness.

The reverse of the electron-positron collision process also happens. A photon of very high energy (not visible, or colored, light, but a very intense X-ray) splits into an electron and a positron. By rotating the diagram counterclockwise ninety degrees, changing the coordinate labels and the arrows, this process can be graphically represented. In this process, too, it was perfectly acceptable to consider only one kind of particle present, an electron. Traveling forward in time the electron appears to have a negative electric charge, and traveling backward in time it appears to have a positive electric charge.*

Feynman's notion suggests that charge is not an invariant property of subatomic particles, but only a term invented by us to indicate their direction of travel in time.

If a photon comes from two like-particles moving differently in time, we might extend our thinking and venture a guess about the nature of a photon's structure. We know that a photon has a wavelike structure. That is, under certain conditions light energy behaves like waves. But the question has always been: "What do light waves wave?" Water waves wave the surface of the water. Sound waves wave air or bone or whatever medium they happen to travel through. But the medium through which light waves usually move is nothing substantial. Light travels fastest in a vacuum. We also know that light waves consist of alternating electric and magnetic fields whose potential varies from negative to positive and back again in a continuous fashion.

Extrapolating from Feynman's ideas we could assume that a light wave vibrates in space-time in such a way that one part lies

*The interactions are somewhat more complex than described here; you can read about them in more detail in Kenneth W. Ford's book, *The World of Elementary Particles,* Blaisdell Press, 1963, or any other text on nuclear physics.

in the future and another part in the past. A light wave exists in the present only on the average. The present, in this description, serves only as a meeting place for the propagating strain which we observe as a light wave or photon.

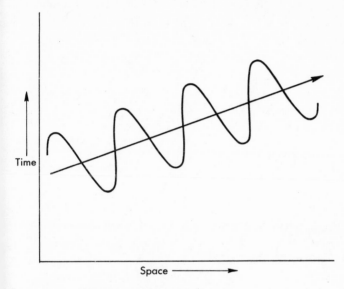

Figure 12. Minkowski diagram of light wave.

Figure 12 illustrates how this might look on a Minkowski diagram.

Some of the future plus some of the past integrate in the present to form a light wave. The system balances and therefore possesses no net electric charge.

If the number of alternations between past and present grows very large per given interval of space-time, the light wave manifests properties which are more particlelike than wavelike. Before this was fully understood people argued whether light was a particle or a wave. Now we recognize that both labels can be applied, depending on the frequency of the light and the conditions of observation. Figure 13 shows the situation wherein the number of alternations is large. Note that the amplitude tapers off at the ends of the wave train. If the wave train is perceived as a whole, i.e., as being particlelike, the ends of the wave train represent the edge of the particle.

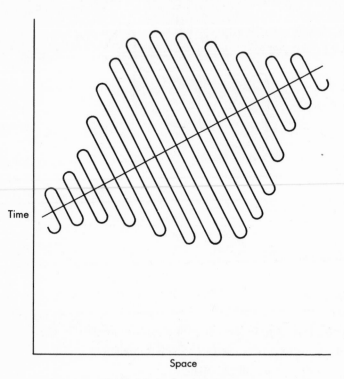

Time

Space

Figure 13. Wave train of particlelike appearance.

It is misleading to label electrons, positrons, and other subatomic "particles" as particles, giving rise to the inference that they are little things—balls of something, sometimes coated with electric charge. They may behave as if they were that way in some interactions, but in other situations and interactions they appear to act more like fields, waves, or distortions in space-time. Since they can be transformed into light waves, which are also distortions in space-time, we may describe an electron or any other particle as a disturbance in space-time, just as a wave is a disturbance of the water's surface. In simpler words, an electron is not a thing, it is a bend in time.

You can visualize this by imagining a line passing along the tops of the waves in Figure 13. This line, looking something like a normal statistical distribution, defines the "particle," but you can readily understand how the term "field" would be just as appropriate, indicating that the presence of the entity extends indefinitely.

Taking the view that an electrical charge arises from direction of movement in time gives us a different picture of what we ordinarily call electrical attraction and repulsion. Due to our limited perception of time as a point-by-point flow, we have invented the notion of positive and negative electric charges to account for the seemingly mysterious "force" of attraction that brings oppositely charged particles together.

However, if we consider a positively charged electron as one kind of distortion in space-time and a negatively charged electron as a symmetric distortion, but in the opposite time direction, we can visualize how the two equal and opposite strains would tend to cancel each other out. If we could perceive space-time all at once, as a static field, we would see that electrons and positrons were simply two sides of the same event. In such a view, electrons and positrons do not attract each other, they simply meet in the "now." By analogy, if we consider magnetic poles as spacelike distortions, it becomes clear why they are not found in isolation; our consciousness of spatial dimensions is extensive and not limited to the now, as is our consciousness of time dimensions. Whenever we "see" one magnetic pole we also "see" the other one because they are coexistent in time. When we "see" an electron, however, we may not immediately "see" its corresponding positron or positive charge because it is not here in this slice of time just now. By and by it will come along. That is, it will become manifest to our perception, to our ordinary consciousness, just as ultraviolet or infrared light is usually invisible but can be made manifest by special devices.

Here we bump into an entirely new limitation of our conception of the universe. Einstein told us that we had a view of space and time limited by the speed of light. Werner Heisenberg showed that we had a fundamental uncertainty in all measurements due to the measuring instrument's effect on what we were looking at, and now we see that we have invented a world view congruent with our limited perception of time. What a dilemma! What is the world really like anyway?

If we consider charged particles as motions or distortions in time, then everything is a net of such distortions. For all substances, all material things consist primarily of electrons and protons in motion. Grass and trees, air and water, even you and I, are simply knots of space and time, kinks in the past and kinks in the future meeting in the now. We meet with each other in the now, each forever instant of the now and only in the now. We are a complex composition of particles meeting, twisting, weaving, wheeling, and spinning from the future into the present and from the past into the present. The very substance of our bodies sums up at once the future and the past—right here, right now. We are of the past, we are of the future, we are here. It is all now in Minkowskian geometry.

Since we don't usually perceive ourselves and others from an extended time or world-line point of view, the notions of time developed by nuclear physicists do not seem to apply to our gross physical bodies. Although the electrons and protons which make up our bodies may be moving to and fro in time, we do not have experiences of moving backward in time or of our bodies ceasing to age. Apparently the reversal of physical time only becomes appreciable for particles moving at speeds near that of light. For a photon or light wave there is no time, but for us, clock time is always flying. These things are confusing to us because we don't yet have a new terminology and new theories for the expanded views of time. Just as in the last couple of chapters I suggested the term "psychological time" for our inner sense of time, now I suggest the term "transcendental time" or perhaps "high time" for the expanded sense of time based upon Minkowski's geometry and the findings of nuclear physicists. Let's see if I can make the notion of transcendental time clearer by more analogies.

Ordinarily we see only a cross section of things as they pass from the world of the future to the world of the past. It is as if we were beings that lived on the surface of water and could perceive only what transpired right at the surface. Any irregular object gliding from the air into the water would appear to us as a two-dimensional something continuously changing its shape. We could not see the whole of the object just as we can't ordinarily see the whole of time. We might think that some "force" acting on the object caused its mysterious changes of shape. Only when the object had passed completely through the surface could we understand the whole of it. Like Alice, our memories only work backward. We invent "forces" and "energies" to substitute for our perceptual limitations of time.

Of course, we do not literally see just a cross section of time. Our consciousness does extend into high time to some degree—if it didn't the world would be just a series of quick flashes. One's nervous system sums up impressions to provide an enduring picture of the environment similar to the way one integrates the static frames of a movie projection to produce the illusion of motion. In the case of the movies we transform static two-dimensional pictures (which represent three-dimensional scenes) into four-dimensional experiences: that is, movement in space during time intervals. In the movies, time is artificially made to flow.

By extension, we can transform a series of movements to give us an experience of world line. An obvious example of world lines are time exposures taken of cars at night. The car lights form streaks (world lines) on the film. Man frequently constructs sections of world lines in his head as he lives his life, and takes no particular notice of this ability. We imagine the path a baseball or frisbee will take in the air, and move to intercept or dodge it; we avoid oncoming cars or pedestrians by plotting their world lines and our own; we plan diagrams or lay out lettering in our heads before committing ourselves to the actual work; and a dozen other things.

We live in high time at least to some extent or we couldn't survive. Nevertheless, we see only a small portion of many world lines, compared to their potential extent. We peep out of a slit of time at the real world which is indifferent to the limitations of our ordinary consciousness. As we raise our consciousness we can begin to see more time-extended views of events. Take a few seconds now to stretch your world view.

Look at some simple objects around you—chairs, desks, lamps, pencils, etc., but instead of just looking at them as simple objects, dwell on each for a brief second and try to perceive it as a four-dimensional object. For instance, visualize the world line of a chair. How long is that particular chair? Visualize the chair in a factory, in a store, in your home, moving from room to room. Visualize the probable future disposition of the chair and imagine its ultimate ending in a fire on a garbage heap somewhere.

What would be the world line of a typewriter? Of the house itself? Try this with different objects you come in contact with whenever you idly walk, drive, or move about. Can you step

above classical space-time to get an expanded sense of the world lines of everything around you?

Although we usually see a person the way we see a physical object, as having definite boundaries, we know that he or she is much more than that. We actually *see* only a time-slice of a person, like a snapshot; by putting many snapshots together we form our view of the person. After all, why should our inner perceptions be limited by the width of our time-slices. Any view of the organism-as-a-whole must be a world-line view to some extent at least, mapped out in four dimensions, not simply a cross-sectional slice.

Consider for example a world line of your physical body. There would be a birth point and a death point about eighty clock years apart; in between, the line would snake back and forth from space point to space point like the most intricate Chinese script, only continually moving upward on the Minkowski plot. Straight vertical lines would represent sleep and periods of quiet, whereas slanting lines would represent motion between space points. You can easily imagine such a world line and you can scan it in a flash as your mind's eye travels along a chain of memories. From such a vantage point you could see all of your life spread out behind you, and in high time you could perceive ahead as well.

Make a deliberate effort to perceive other persons as world lines, all at once, spread out before your mental eyes. Blur their physical image into an extended lifeline. Recall their past and imagine their future. Blend the past and future together into one line image. Now visualize yourself as a world line. How does your world line intertwine with those of others? What's this trip like that you're on?

Although we have been taught to believe that our organisms move through time, in a four-dimensional geometry there would be no motion in time. We just are—long, living lines stretched out between two points, one called "birth" and the other "death." With such a conception birth and death are merely end points of a totality; from a timeless point of view the whole exists at once.

To see this clearly I must place my viewing point outside of space-time. I must transcend the simple here-now awareness of the ongoing present and try to take a bigger view, as a hiker does when he reaches a hilltop and looks back at his path or forward to his destination. The greater the degree of my consciousness, the more of the path behind and ahead come into my view.

An ant, crawling on the tabletop cannot see where it has been or where it is going. It is forced to crawl over the two-dimensional surface one point at a time. It has scarcely more than a two-dimensional consciousness. We humans, with our mobility in three dimensions and our sense of sight, can comprehend the two-dimensional table at a glance, take in the path of the ant, and predict its destination. With one time-exposure photograph we could capture a segment of his world line. Would that we could see ourselves as we see the ant!

As it is now, we have only the most feebly developed higher consciousness, just as lower animals possess only the most weakly developed time sense. Occasionally, though, we do have snatches of awareness which transcend space-time and leave us breathless with awe. In such brief instants one may have views of "the future" or be struck with an intense emotional awareness of one's whole life, its meaning, purpose, and direction. Ordinarily this happens rarely, our vision is blurred and confounded by a thousand fantasies and imaginings—wishes, hopes, and desires.

Perhaps this represents the first edge of an evolutionary advance. For if consciousness acts as the driving force of evolution, as Teilhard de Chardin suggests, then consciousness of time provides a significant measure of our evolutionary growth both as a species and as individuals.

Each level of life encompasses and transcends the lower ones in its freedom to move in space and time. Plants have only the most limited knowledge of the space dimension. They can only move about by transforming their essence into seed form and relocating it elsewhere, that is by "dying" and being "reborn" in another place. Animals can move freely in space, although they have much less time consciousness than man. They transcend time only by death and rebirth.

Men were born to the freedom of land space, have covered sea space, and now even pushed into extraterrestrial space. The next frontier lies in the dimensions of time. Consciousness of time arose early in man's history—a time based on the sun's rising and setting and the season's changes. The development of spoken, and especially written language have enabled man to leapfrog through time, building idea upon idea, generation after generation, in a continual progression. Moreover, his conceptualization of time and its measure have refined and sharpened; today's standards of clock time represent a nearly ultimate degree of precision. But as we have seen, the rigidity of clock time does not fit our inner consciousness, or does it apply to phenomena on the frontiers of science. We have simultaneously arrived in both science and psychology at the need for developing new ways of conceptualizing and perceiving time. In our present stage of development, we are confused by the amphibious nature of our existence, with its occasional exhaltation at the spiritual level of high time, and its daily struggle to satisfy our animal needs. We are like pioneers in a new land, a land with few trails and only rudimentary maps. Clearly we need guidelines for our spiritual growth. The notions I have developed from science show that solid foundations are available to help focus our experiences and make them comprehensible. Perhaps these ideas will make it easier to understand those superpsychiatrists and gurus, who have advanced two or three steps in consciousness, who seek to help us along the pathways of evolution.

MOMENT

Now, starflake frozen on the windowpane
All of a winter night, the open hearth
Blazing beyond Andromeda, the sea-
Anemone and the downwind seed, O moment
Hastening, halting in a clockwise dust,
The time in all hospitals is now,
Under the arc-lights where the sentry walks
His lonely wall it never moves from now,
And now is quiet in the tomb as now
Explodes inside the sun, and it is now
In the saddle of space, where argosies of dust
Sail outward blazing, and mind of God,
The flash across the gap of being, thinks
In the instant absence of forever: now!

—HOWARD NEMEROV

| XI |

A Fifth Dimension

"Which reminds me———" the White Queen said, looking
down nervously clasping and unclasping her hands, "we had
such a thunderstorm last Tuesday———I mean one of the last
set of Tuesdays, you know."

Alice was puzzled. "In *our* country," she remarked,
"there's only one day at a time."

The Red Queen said "That's a poor thin way of doing
things. Now *here,* we mostly have days and nights two or
three at a time, and sometimes in the winter we take as
many as five nights together———for warmth you know."

—LEWIS CARROLL

The awareness of our lives as continuous four-dimensional world
lines will not enable us to transcend time at the physical level.
We cannot travel backward, grow young again, step into the
future, or avoid death. Our ordinary consciousness must still
travel along our world lines, from one point to another, enclosed
in the three-dimensional temples of our bodies and the protective
coatings of our acquired personalities.

Although our bodies are inserted into time and space and
constrained to follow the ruts of linear clock time, our

consciousness flies free in high time. Mentation, operating in the framework of psychological time, roams easily throughout the real and imaginary universe. The future, the past, and the imaginary merge, integrated by the process of mentation. Our present actions operate as an integrated or synthesized function of the past and the future (as we perceive or imagine it). What I am doing now depends on the coming of night, on the inevitable dinner, on a future series of events about the publishing of this book, on my work with these ideas begun fifteen years ago, as well as my rough outline of five years ago. All these factors integrate into my present functioning, writing, and behavior.

Mentation requires some clock time, and is presumably always associated with organs that are spatial and that function in clock time; but memory, as a type of mentation, carries one backward in time and enables one to view the present as the future; imagination transcends space-time enabling one to see the "there" as "here," and the "then" as "now." We can imagine something from tomorrow just as easily as we can imagine something from Mars. We can imagine what might have happened just as easily as what might happen. We can imagine anything, anywhen. In a flash we can think of a distant star, a past event, a future lover, or an imaginary cartoon character.

How can we construct a model of consciousness that will take into account a man's mind? A model that will handle several simultaneous events, transcend space-time, account for our inner lives, and cover the whole of the real and imaginary universe? Four-dimensional world lines, however complex they become, still seem weak simplifications of our actual needs.

In building our model, let's consider some simple premises. For every simultaneously occurring event of the present, our corporeal world line may branch out in several different directions, each one representing a different future. Whatever is happening right now sets up the conditions for what happens next. Each moment, each event overflows with potential, with unmanifest possibilities so great that we can scarcely survey them all. At every here-now instant, a dozen future possibilities exist and each of them, if actualized, could lead to another dozen, and so on indefinitely. The range of alternatives for every proposed action defies any easy comprehension.

We continually select what we want to do or what we must do from all the things we might do. The more conscious we are, the better our choices turn out.

In a strict sense we perceive only a little bit of the extension of our world line into what we call the future. We survey more than one world line, however; for choosing implies alternatives and each alternative represents another world line.

Consider the game of chess. Each move offers a new beginning point for every piece on the board. Only one piece moves at a time, but the potential exists for a very large number of moves. If we kept track of all the moves of all the pieces during the game we could easily draw a world line for each piece. For all the actual world lines for each piece a vastly larger number of unmanifest world lines arise from moves that might have been made. These unmanifest world lines are not real in the sense of having physical existence, but they are real to our mental perception (at least some of them are—depending on our chess-playing abilities). Any full view of reality must consider the important reality that exists in your head and mine, for our total reality consists solely of both manifest and unmanifest world lines.

In a way, our lives resemble a giant game of chess. For every position, every condition, we have a vast number of potential moves. Each moment serves as the seed of a new beginning, a new branching-off point. What will happen? What will we do? Where will we go? Truly it has been said that "Today is the first day of the rest of your life."

A Minkowski diagram, including potential world lines as well as the manifest ones, would consist of continuously branching lines like a forever growing tree (Figure 14).

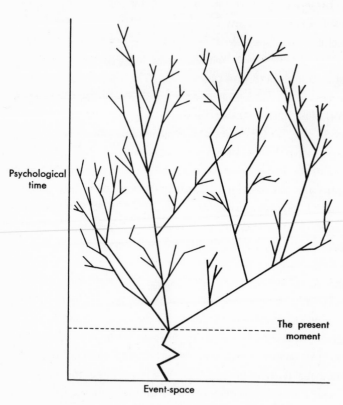

Figure 14. Possible world lines beginning from the present.

As the consciousness directs the body into one world line rather than another, either by chance or the pressure of events, the potential world lines fade away leaving only the actualized line.

Perceiving potential world lines might come naturally to the

Hopi, for they are accustomed to sensing the unmanifest at the core of every living and nonliving thing, an unmanifest that includes wishes, hopes, fears, growth, or imaginary actions. As nearly as I can understand it at second hand, the Hopi view "now" as the point at which the unmanifest switches over to the manifest—where alternate world lines dissolve.

This point is not an objective, absolute point-in the universe, but is relative to our senses and our ordinary consciousness, to what we can see with our limited perception of time. Because the Hopi do not have a piecemeal view of time such as ours, they see things more as a whole, with an extension from what we call the past to the future, both real and imaginary.

The Hopi probably also see more clearly how things and events overlap and cross-couple, forming a complicated network of world lines. If we could draw a super Minkowski diagram which was more representative of our actual living experience it might look like Figure 15.

This figure looks like the neural interconnections within the brain, and is in fact a drawing of a portion of the visual cortex by Ramon y Cajal. As described in Chapter IX, each happening, each sensation, comes to the brain as a pattern of neural impulses that travels along the neurons on many parallel pathways. These minute electrical currents flowing through the branching dendrites and axons of each nerve cell literally *are* our awareness of the world. Their moving patterns constitute our "trip," our Minkowski world lines in psychological space-time.

Our ordinary consciousness generally flows down only one world line at a time, but in a fifth dimensional view each world line would represent a different little "i" of consciousness. At each branching point consciousness splits into different portions or "i's" which see the world differently, and each of these "i's" may subdivide still further, coming together for a while, only to split once again.

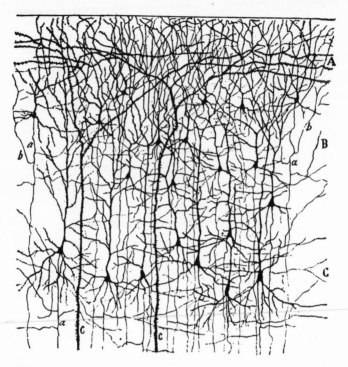

Figure 15. Network of world lines in the brain.

Something catches my eye out of the window. Initially i_1 was typing. Now i_2 begins an if-trip about raking the yard. I_1 continues typing, faltering now and then. I_3 enters, laying a guilt-trip on i_2 for letting the yard go to such chaos. I_1 takes over, squelches the rest, and continues typing forcibly. But after a few minutes i_4 enters, demanding food, or rest, and so it goes all day long.

If I am lost in one particular train of thought to the exclusion of others, then all the energy of my consciousness flows into that one train, along that one world line. If I am in a more observant mood, the little sub-"i's" come and go, with no one of them taking precedence over the rest. Consciousness roams freely through the neural network, although the exact manner in which this occurs is not yet known by science. If we are in a negative, critical, or pessimistic state, consciousness will be forced to one side of the mainstream, and all neural trips will occur on that side (psychological, not necessarily physical) of the brain.

We will be prevented from apprehending the other side of things. We may be equally forced to the opposite side by too positive an evaluation. We have been brought up to believe that we must do one thing at a time. When a struggle to think several things at once occurs we usually force ourselves to pick one to the exclusion of the others, or, if we are weak-willed, our mind veers off on its own. Our mentation process seesaws back and forth, creating continual inner turmoil and strife. The battle of ''i's'' rages unceasingly, even in our so-called sleep. Meditation and alpha training can help you rise above this battle, as can practice in attending to the here-now. Both techniques rest the mind. The former raises consciousness, the latter steadies it.

Each little ''i'' of mentation takes me down a branch, a world line, a neural pathway. Each awareness of something happening here-now brings me back to a main trunk. If a strong thought seizes my consciousness, it may grow far from the main trunk. If most of my mental, physical, or emotional energy goes into it, it may become even stronger and grow very far from here-now reality. Soon, my thoughts (if not my entire organism) will be out of balance. My health may suffer, neurotic or psychotic symptoms may arise. I may get out of touch with ''reality''; if I am entirely on my own trip others may call me crazy. Sanity is a cultural average of everyone's neural trips. Depression, self-rejection, paranoia, or other delusions take hold of most people to some degree now and then. When I am here-now with what is happening, energy is drawn out of these side branches and consciousness returns to the main trunk.

This process is analogous to waking from a bad dream. In a dream, consciousness is weak and one is temporarily caught up in a threatening, painful, or destructive thought train. Suddenly, one wakes and realizes that it is 6 A.M., the new day is beginning, and the room is cold. The dream fades quickly, replaced by sensory input from the here-now, the security of bed and home and daylight and other people. To a lesser, but more subtle extent we slip in and out of dreams all day long. The little sub-"i's" keep in touch with what is happening. When we can summon up a degree of impartiality and are in touch with the higher consciousness, the entire set of if-trips, of alternate world lines, appears as a whole.

We can get a crude model of this if we visualize a Minkowski-like diagram of the patterns of neural impulses flowing through our brains from birth to death. Such a diagram would be a total map of our psychological life.

Picture something like a long strip of movie film taken from one individual's birth to his death, in which each frame shows the electrical pattern active in the neurons for that particular slice of time. By looking at any frame of the film strip, we could see what neural pattern was energized and interpret the individual's experience at that particular moment. His whole life would be present to our eyes, every experience recorded as a neural pattern on the film strip.

How could we tell from the neural patterns which ones represented real experience and which ones denoted unmanifest if-trips? While the physical body may be constrained to follow one path or world line, the inner neural world is not; many neural pathways may be energized simultaneously. How do we know which one is "real" in the sense of having been generated from outside the organism? As in a statistical distribution, perhaps the most highly energized neural pathways represent the manifest while the others fade away into degrees of unmanifestation (similar to the time distribution of here-now described in Chapter III).

Speculations on simultaneous world lines and maps of the neural cortex may appear strange to psychologists, but not to the physicist engaged in studying the realm of subatomic particles. Figure 16, reproduced from the cover of Kenneth Ford's book *The World of Elementary Particles*, shows how a proton (nucleus of a hydrogen atom) may travel different world-lines or disintegrate

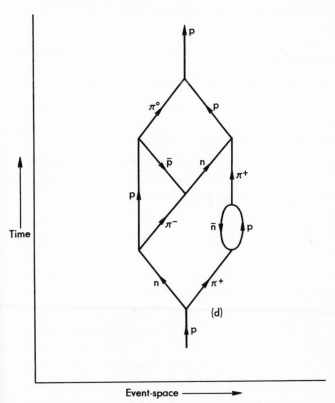

Figure 16. Potential world lines for a single proton.

into different kinds of particles, finally reintegrating into a proton again. The reintegration ultimately takes place because the proton must follow the law of conservation of energy, just as our physical organism must ultimately follow one time line. In the drawing the other symbols represent particles which are called "virtual" because their existence is transitory.

In other words, different possibilities of existence are open to the proton. A proton does not necessarily undergo this complex path, it may follow a simpler one, by temporarily disintegrating into a neutron (n) and a positive pion (π^+). But the possibilities still exist, just as they do for you and for me.

For example, right now you can sense some of the possibilities for the next moment. You could stop reading. You could go eat any one of many foods. You could pick up another book, etc. Each one of these possibilities would lead to a different set of activities, though eventually they might all cease at the end of the day when going to sleep.

The set of different future possibilities starting from this instant could conceivably be ordered along a dimension of probability. Such an ordered set would constitute a "fifth" dimension beyond the first three dimensions of space and the fourth of time.

Consider a roll of dice as an example. The roll may turn up any one of twenty-one possible sums. There can be a 1–1, a 1–2, a 1–3 . . .; a 2–2, a 2–3, a 2–4, and so on. We can calculate the different possibilities of rolling the dice such that the sum of the faces equals seven or five or two or twelve, etc., and we could put all the different scores in the order based on their probabilities. This would define a fifth dimension for the dice positions.

We can draw a modified Minkowski diagram for the potential world lines of the dice. The probability of obtaining a 7 is the most likely combination for it will occur six times out of thirty-six rolls (on the average). This event would be the main world line, that is, the one most apt to become manifest. The probability of rolling a 6 or an 8 equals 5/36, the next most likely event. The chance of rolling snake eyes or crocodiles (two 1s or two 6s) is only 2/36 and these events would be represented by the most divergent world lines. Figure 17 depicts this event-space.

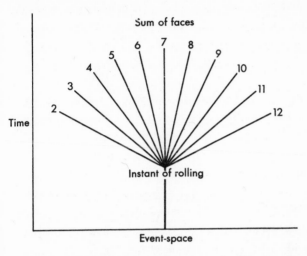

Figure 17. Modified Minkowski diagram of rolling two dice.

To get a better feel for what I mean by a five-dimensional space, imagine drawing a whole set of Minkowski diagrams each one containing only one of the many alternative possibilities. Then give a probability-of-occurrence measure to each different diagram and stack them one on top of the other in order of the probability of occurrence. (You could also stack them symmetrically up and down with the most probable world line in the middle of the stack.) This ordered stack of four-dimensional diagrams would constitute a fifth dimension analogous to the way a stack of two-dimensional sheets of paper constitutes a three-dimensional solid.

159   A Fifth Dimension

Each potential direction of our lives has a certain indefinite probability of becoming manifest. We cannot calculate exact numbers in most cases because our lives are too complex, and because our actions frequently depend on the indeterminate actions of others. However, we can make reasonable guesstimates of many future events and we certainly can give clear outside boundaries in most cases. There are limits in rolling dice and in life. You can't roll a pair of sevens with the usual six-sided dice. You can't expect a dandelion to turn into a rose, or your imaginary Uncle Remus to leave you a real million dollars.

You may have heard the story about the tourist who asked a drunk for directions in downtown Boston, which is notorious for its twisting, winding streets. "First," said the drunk, "you go down this street, and turn left, then . . . No!" he interrupted himself. "That won't work. Go up here to the third light, then turn right, then left again, then go . . . no, no, that won't work either . . . . OK, go this way [he pointed up the street]. . . . No, that won't work either." After a long pause he finally exclaimed, "Mister, you just can't get there from here!"

Our future possibilities are not limitless; they are infinite, but the laws and principles of physics and chemistry set certain ground rules and boundary conditions for us, as do biology, and our psychosocial and economic environments.

Death, the mixing of materials, the aging of cells, success and failures—all these will happen with greater or lesser probability as our physical organisms move from point to point through space-time. If all probabilities were 1, that is, were certainties, we would have only one Minkowski diagram containing only one world line. Our lives would be completely predetermined. But all future events are not certainties. There are probabilities that we will be cast into certain events, rather than others. We live in a five-dimensional world, not simply a four-dimensional one. Lower animals do not clearly recognize causal relations among events. The robot and the computer do not live in time, for they blindly obey the programs humans put into them, and react to stimuli in a predetermined fashion. Consciousness of time awakens when one is faced with a choice. The greater the consciousness the more choice one has, the more "time" one can perceive.

It is this field of manifold possibilities of action—branching from every instant that you may become aware of as you proceed from simple here-now awareness toward the state of cosmic consciousness—that I called the transcendental here-now.

If you can be here-now with a simple object, with your thoughts, feelings, or actions—if you can be aware of the way in which the ordinary past comes into the active present, and if you can, at the same instant, comprehend at least some of the manifest possibilities of actions and events, you will be at least partially in the transcendental here-now, in an awareness that is beyond time and space as you have learned to know it, an awareness of your existence as a conscious being in a fifth dimension.

As we become more conscious, i.e., as we learn to live more in the fifth dimension, we gain more freedom. We can choose, within limits, where we want to go. As the saying goes, "We get on top of things."

I am not trying to prove the existence of free will, but assuming its existence and showing how it comes as a natural consequence of a five-dimensional description of our lives. Classical physics stopped at a four-dimensional view of the world and such a viewpoint has created a conflict with our ordinary experience of volition and consciousness. Modern physics has laid the groundwork for a five-dimensional view which helps clarify the linguistic dichotomy of free will versus determinism.

Five-dimensional structures give us the possibilities of choice, of will, and hence of higher consciousness. Cause, effect, and determinism are only aspects of the whole. They are useful linguistic splits only in a four-dimensional universe. Man is not in such a universe, he lives beyond it. Nevertheless, free will is not "free"; it takes effort to operate in the fifth dimension, chained as we are by our own "un"-consciousness.

From a five-dimensional point of view the future is not a single world, but a matrix of events or a set of alternative possibilities. We have the freedom to move among different world lines; we are not necessarily predestined to move only along certain prescribed paths.

Perhaps consciousness could be defined as the degree of inner freedom we have. The higher the consciousness, the more freedom we have to move five-dimensionally.

If our consciousness lowers through illness, despair, or idleness we will naturally and inevitably fall into the easiest or most probable world lines. We won't have much freedom and we will come under the influence of others (or of the "stars" which some say are conscious beings controlling life on earth for their ends and not ours). Moreover, negative emotions or hidden factors in our own make-up may subtly direct us along unpleasant world lines. Ignorance, coupled with diminished consciousness, may be directing us down the wrong bunny trail, and we may have about as much awareness of it as a bunny! If we have acquired a gloomy or destructive set, we may always be taking wrong branches of our world lines, unaware that choice is possible.

Here is where a psychiatrist or friend can straighten us out. A little effort, a little knowledge, and the insight of another person can help us develop our freedom of choice. We can resist the "forces of time" and redirect our destinies.

We do this to some degree when we deliberately decide which

movie to go to, which item on the menu to order, which route to take driving home, and so on.

Perhaps you use this faculty of choice without really considering how wonderful and unique it is. No animal can operate with the ease in which we can, or choose one from many imagined alternatives before acting. Perhaps, too, you misuse this faculty. i have often observed myself if-tripping in my head along one unmanifest world line while my body moves along a different one. Such un-here-nowness results in a split between mind and body, leading to all sorts of difficulties which you probably have encountered now and then in your own life. I'm convinced that many accidents stem from daydreaming, as well as from overeating, muscular tensions, eye strain, headaches, or backaches. If I leave my body unattended for very long, who knows what might happen? Something could even steal it!

Such schizoid behavior is very prevalent in our ototoverbal, head-oriented culture. As stressed in earlier chapters, the pathway to higher consciousness lies through the body, not in absent-minded, unconscious, or even deliberate detachment from it.

Try to get a strong sense of the here-now as a prerequisite for the next couple of exercises. Try to get a feeling of being all together at one point on your four-dimensional world line, then stretch your awareness to encompass a five-dimensional view.

> **Sit quietly for a minute and try to get a sense of yourself sitting. Then try to be aware of all the activities or things that are happening in, through, and around you. Extend your awareness into the past as far as you can for each event. How old is that music you hear? Where did it come from? How did it enter your life? What about that picture on the wall? What were its origins? How long has it been there? What about the tree that helped make this book possible? Where did it come from?**
>
> **Then turn your attention to what is possible for each thing or**

happening, to the unmanifest potential of each one. How much can you perceive? How much can you imagine? Can you get a sense of the many realities in which you exist and how much freedom of movement you actually have?

It's a little bit like being on a high mountain peak—you can go down off the peak in many different directions. The higher the peak, the more clearly you can see the terrain around you, and the more potential for movement you have.

Try a similar expansion of perception with other persons. In the previous chapter I asked you to "see" others as world lines rather than discrete entities. Now expand upon that exercise, looking upon other persons (and yourself, or course) as networks of world lines.

First, Look at others as five-dimensional shapes. Try to visualize the activities of the person as stretched out and visible to your eyes. Conceptualize his world lines passing through and connected with his experiences and happenings. Now imagine his branching points and potential possibilities. If you could see inside his brain, see his inner ventures, his manifold of if-trips, plans worries, and dreams; and if those were visible as some kind of shape, how would he look? What would be his total five-dimensional shape?

A human being is an incredibly complex structure!

To view human consciousness as operating from a five-dimensional framework makes it easier to understand the occurrence of psi phenomena such as clairvoyance, telepathy, or telekinesis. We all can predict a little distance into the future in most situations. We take steps to safeguard our lives and property when we cross a busy street, shop at a store, plan for a mountain climb, prepare for a storm, and so on. We regard this behavior as perfectly natural, so why shouldn't a clairvoyant or prophet who is a little more future-sighted also be taken as ordinary and natural? Perhaps five-dimensional vision lies only a degree beyond our ordinary ability, its use hampered by our restricted notion of time, our belief that we can't see into the future which is, by definition, an unknowable place. Our very use of the noun "future" gives the impression that it is a definite place completely different from "now" or "the present" which are also terms with a connotation of definiteness, entirely contrary to the facts.

We all see far and near into the future now and then. You've probably had the experience of strongly feeling that something was about to happen just before it occurred. Have you also had the experience of going to some new place and suddenly getting the feeling that you have been there before? This experience occurs so frequently that it has been given the French term *déjà vu*.

Perhaps you've had prophetic visions or dreams of the future which were later fulfilled, or may know someone who has such dreams or visions. Usually we don't talk much about such "weird" happenings, for fear people may think we are a little crazy.

Just the same, many persons by chance or accident reach a higher level of consciousness where they do see into the future, or at least some portion of it. Moreover, the future they perceive is not always rigidly determined. Hundreds of people have reported prophetic dreams, voices, or visions which warned them against certain actions or away from certain situations. They have been able, in many cases, to willfully choose another world line or path of action, to avoid injury or death, such as from a train wreck, poisoned food, or falling objects. Clearly, they did perceive one aspect of the unmanifest, one world line, one event from the so-called future, and redirected their course along a different world line, just as we would step out of the way of an oncoming car.

Why do clairvoyant perceptions so often come as visions, dreams, or even voices? We don't know; perhaps the situation is analogous to our present way of handling subconscious information. Feelings or thoughts which are buried in the subconscious because they would be unacceptable to the ordinary consciousness, often seek expression in dreams, peculiar behavior, and sometimes voices, as Freud and later psychologists have observed. To many people, seeing into the future is considered impossible or taboo. They won't allow perceptions of the future to enter into their brains undistorted; so the superconscious is forced to reveal its contents by roundabout methods. As we are superpsychoanalyzed by our gurus we will probaby find clairvoyance a perfectly acceptable fact of our existence. Once we acknowledge a different conception of time, we will not need to be so bound by calendars, clocks, and customs. We can resensitize ourselves to a wider view of reality and accept our "out of time" experiences and clairvoyant perceptions as natural abilities too long dormant and unused.

The same notions apply to the other psi abilities. In the phenomena of telekinesis, for instance, individuals move or influence objects in their motion by purely "mental means." A person possessing this psi ability may cause clock hands to rotate, dice to fall a certain way, objects to fall to the floor, etc. How people perform these feats remain a mystery. Perhaps they are able to choose what world line they will move along or to jump abruptly from one world line to another. For example, they may be able to choose a world line wherein the dice will always roll up sevens. Perhaps telekinesis is not the ability to move objects, but to bend world lines. Although this may sound a bit strange, it is actually congruent with Einstein's theory that gravitation is our name for bent world lines in Minkowski space. That is, an object does not attract other objects to it by some mysterious "force of gravitational attraction"; rather, it bends the Minkowski world lines in the local space-time region. It follows from this that "gravity" would affect time rate, which has been experimentally verified. It seems natural to hypothesize that a similar structural change in the world lines might account for psychokinesis, and that, somehow, gravity and consciousness are linked. After all, gravity is the most cohesive "force" in the universe, pulling all matter together so that other, more complex evolutionary changes can occur. If we look closely at the operation of the brain, taking into account higher consciousness and five-dimensional freedom, we bump right into telekinesis. For instance, how do I actually initiate an action? If I am quietly meditating and then decide to speak or make some simple gesture, how is this brought about at the lowest structural level? We know that any thought corresponds with a movement of electrons in the excitation of neurons within my brain. But what moves these electrons along one course rather than another? If I decide to open my right eye and not my left one, how is this decision made? How are electrical impulses directed to the muscles controlling my right eye only? What if I choose to expand upon a thought that comes into my consciousness about getting the car fixed? What activates those neural circuits rather than some other set? These functions are no chance affairs; consciousness directs our actions. How exactly does it operate?

As I explained for biofeedback training in Chapter VI, the brain acts like an amplifier. The most minute thoughts can be amplified into the greatest actions and amplified even further by modern technology. A man can throw a switch or push a button and set up a chain of actions that can blow the top off a mountain or launch a spaceship. A modern transistor needs only one millionth of a volt to turn it on. A few electrons, when amplified by transistors, can direct the flow of many amperes along one pathway or another. Perhaps our brains can amplify signals far smaller than one millionth of a volt. But what are the signals? Where do they arise? What gives them the initial impetus?

I suggest that something like telekinesis or the ability to move electrons takes place within the brain. At this level, our higher consciousness, operating from a fifth dimension, acts on the gross, highly complex electrochemistry of the brain. The effect may be minute, but it is real. True choice of action exists, however weak and hemmed in it may be.

Since electrons are bends in space-time, that is five-dimensional knots, perhaps it is sloppy language to say that consciousness "acts on" the brain. For, from a five-dimensional viewpoint, consciousness simply is, and is everywhere at once. Maybe the brain serves merely as a link from the fifth dimension to the fourth one, like a kind of transformer. In the same way, our physical bodies serve to transform the brain processes into the third dimension.

Ordinarily we do not have much free will—our brains and bodies generate so much internal noise and react in so mechanical a fashion to external stimuli that the effect of higher consciousness is nearly swamped out. Nevertheless, it is said that higher consciousness is always operating and if conditions are favorable its presence will become manifest.

In a strictly neural sense then, our higher consciousness directs our course along one (or perhaps millions) neural pathway rather than others. That is, it directs us along one particular world line. We might well say that, like gravity, higher consciousness bends world lines. To the extent that we "tune in" to our higher consciousness we allow our own destinies to be guided.

If we consider the brain as a delicate amplifier for signals emanating from a five-dimensional continuum (signals comprising a different form of energy; gravitational, perhaps, rather than electromagnetic), then telepathy may be simply the receptivity of one amplifier to the signals emanating from another. Research on alpha rhythms and telepathy is inconclusive at the present time (1972), but it seems to indicate that a person is more receptive when he is quiet and in the alpha state. Many instances of telepathy occur in crises situations between people who have shared strong emotional or informational channels of communication. Telepathy seems rare between complete strangers. Perhaps brain amplifiers need to be somehow attuned to each other. As we commonly say: "He and I are on the same wave length."

Research on psi phenomena and other psychic abilities is being carried out in many laboratories around the world. The development of sophisticated electronic equipment for measuring brain waves and other internal states has been accompanied by a more open and inquiring state of mind among many scientists, and we can expect new discoveries to be made in abundance in the next few years.

The greatest need at the present time is for the development of a useful theory which makes psi phenomena and other psychic abilities sensible, logical, and describable. Many of these phenomena are considered "unexplainable" because they defy our established conventions of space-time and causation. By formulating events in a five-dimensional framework and hypothesizing a higher human consciousness which operates in such a dimension, many miracles become describable. I can't prove that my formulations are the correct and proper ones. There are plenty of gaps in my ideas and my understanding, and many scientific measurements are still to be made. But perhaps these notions will serve as a starting point to guide others to develop more appropriate and more detailed notions. It is up to you to construct your own modifications as you try the exercises. Whatever you think, it is more than that!

. . . . . .

All is illusion, say the cynics and the sages—a statement which carries a note of despair. When we perceive reality in terms of five-dimensional world lines and alternate neural networks, however, the outlook changes entirely. At any given moment the world may appear unalterable and tragic to our veiled eyes, but with expanded consciousness we can recognize that this single, apparent, concrete reality is but one of many possible forms. With the right kind of "vision," other possibilities emerge alongside our simple here-now, and may lend the here-now a somewhat insubstantial quality, like virtual particles in subatomic physics. The manifest and the unmanifest are not dichotomous states, but blend indivisibly into a continuous whole, merging into a field of excitation in our neural cortex. If one reaches this state of awareness through drugs or artificial means or by some happenstance, without concomitant understanding, we may become confused or disoriented. These other realities, these other world lines, spreading and tumbling all through and around one, may submerge the reality usually identified as the main one, leaving us with the feeling that reality is illusionary and transitory. From a five-dimensional view, however, each reality is as valid as any other. Only our perception is limited. When we break through our neural conditioning, we may welcome the infusion of other realities into the main reality. Such a view leads to a renewed interest in living, not to despair, for the multidimensional reality is much richer than a linear, one-track world.

> All of a person's reality is just neurons
> Lighting up and dying down.
> Flicker, flicker, flicker . . .
> Like piles and piles of Christmas trees
> With miles and miles of winking, blinking lights.
> No wonder you are such a twinkle in my eye!

3

TRANSCENDING "I"

*Our culture is based upon a false
assumption about the nature of man. We
are programed to believe that on one
side is man with his artificial food, ticky
tacky boxes, automobiles, and his whole
plastic way of life, while on the other
exists the world of nature—trees,
mountains, flowers, rivers, lakes, and all
the animal species. Such elementalistic
thinking sets man apart from the world
and men apart from each other. To be
shut off from others and the world,
alone and turned inward, is the curse of
our age. Alienation is a lie we have
swallowed whole.*

*Current scientific knowledge leads
directly to the recognition that we are
physically and biologically connected to
each other and to the entire universe.
When this recognition becomes intuitive
and direct it has been called "revelation"
or enlightenment and the experience is
described as one of "mystical oneness."
There is nothing mystical about it,
however; it is only an accident of our
biology that we perceive separateness.
Just as we are color-blind to infrared*

light, so are we unaware of the reality of our togetherness. Modern science has given us extra neural means of "seeing" the full nature of ourselves and our unity with the world. In this section I pass on some of these scientific perceptions to you so that your understanding will be deepened.

Modern science also provides us with a logical base from which to account for eternal life, reincarnation, and related beliefs which have heretofore been relegated to religion or to "crackpots" on the fringes. In this section I give some broad outlines from which a theory might be derived. Nothing can be proved—yet. But the history of science shows that experimental findings are seldom accepted until some kind of credible theory is formulated which makes sense to our rational minds. Or, to put it differently: our minds need stretching and expanding before we will believe and accept with our hearts the evidence of our own experience. Therefore—read on!

XII

The We Field

"How can there be such a thing as the end of time?" said
Alice.

"How can there be such a thing as the end of you?"
snapped the Turtle snootily.

"Of course," thought Alice, "a turtle would say that
because he was so round," but she didn't say anything
because she wanted to hurry on to the next square."

The notion of objects or persons as a network of world lines
becomes cumbersome when we examine it in detail. The world
lines for even a simple object are so finely partitioned and
interwoven that a line drawing of them would look like a fuzzy
blur. Here again we can borrow from the terminology of the
physicist and refer to the manifold possibilities and overlapping
event-processes of "things" and "person" as *fields,* rather than
as discrete patterns of world lines.

Introduced into physics by Michael Faraday and James C.
Maxwell in the nineteenth century, the field was first considered
to be merely a mathematical construct—an alternate way of
describing the observed behavior of charged particles. Every
electrically charged particle supposedly possessed a field

surrounding it and emanating from it. By drawing radical lines emanating from the particle in all directions, the strength of the field at a given point was determined by the magnitude of the charge on the particle and its distance from the particle. Besides electrical fields, particles were also presumed to have gravitational fields, magnetic fields, and, in some cases, nuclear fields.

Scientists soon recognized electric and magnetic fields as being different aspects of the same event. Hence the term "electromagnetic field" came into use. Later, Einstein attempted to heal the split between electromagnetism and gravity with his unified-field theory. With the development of field notions, space and time eventually came to be considered as a "fullness" of fields, all blended together; space-time is just another way of saying "electromagnetic-gravitational field." Where spacelike distortions are called magnetic, timelike distortions are called electric and distortions of world lines of particles toward each other are called gravitation.

The term "field," originally introduced as a convenient abstraction, has now come to refer to an actual physical reality. Gradually the notion of concrete, distinct, solitary particles which moved through space carrying their fields with them like furry blankets has been replaced by the realization that fields best describe the basic entities out of which particles become manifest to our crude instruments of observation, limited means of perception, and linguistic representation. What we formerly thought to be discrete particles simply mark the place where the field or the distortion of space-time are the greatest. The term "particle" serves as a mere approximation—a distorted categorization of the physical world. It is as if we had taken a statistical distribution, drawn a line for the mean, and then said that the mean line formed the whole of it, ignoring the rest of the distribution.

Furthermore, from a field point of view, every field-particle interacts with every other field-particle (whatever happens at one point is felt throughout the field). The fields merge, blend, focus, and weave together. Formerly we restricted our attention only to the knots (particles), ignoring the fibers themselves. Physicist Kenneth Ford wrote:

> A particle is just fields in interaction, its mass and other "intrinsic" properties are not really intrinsic at all, but arise from the interactions of this particle with all other particles, . . . the form of those interactions, in turn, being dictated by conservation laws. Because of the phenomenon of self-interaction, the being and the happening are inseparable ideas. This is a new element in the scientist's view of the world, an element that has been present only for about the past thirty years. Its importance is likely to increase.*

Such a field view of the subatomic universe seems foreign, and difficult for us to understand only because we have grown up with an elementalistic and antiquated language structure, which worked perfectly well for the simple physical world of two thousand years ago, but which is unfit for today's known universe. Benjamin Whorf saw this very clearly. Twenty-five years before Ford, he pointed out that the meaning of an electron depends on its context. He wrote:

> Just as language consists of discrete lexation-segmentation and ordered patternment, of which the latter has the more background character, less obvious but more infrangible and universal, so the physical world may be an aggregate of quasi-discrete entities (atoms, crystals, living organisms, planets, stars, etc.) not fully understandable as such, but rather emergent from a field of causes that is itself a manifold of pattern and order. It is upon the bars of the fence, beyond which it would meet these CHARACTERS OF THE FIELD, that science is now poised. As physics explores into the intra-atomic phenomena, the discrete physical forms and forces are more and more dissolved into relations of pure patternment. The PLACE of an apparent entity, an

* *The World of Elementary Particles,* p. 215.

electron for example, becomes indefinite, interrupted; the entity appears and disappears from one structural position to another structural position, like a phenomena or any other patterned linguistic entity, and may be said to be NOWHERE in between positions. Its locus, first thought of and analyzed as a continuous variable, becomes on closer scrutiny a mere alternation; situations "actualize" it, structure beyond the probe of the measuring rod governs it; three-dimensional shape, there is none,—instead—"Arupa" (higher dimensional patternment).

Science cannot yet understand the transcendental logic of such a state of affairs, for it has not yet freed itself from the illusory necessities of common logic which are at bottom only necessities of grammatical pattern in Western Aryan grammar, necessities for substantives in certain sentence positions, necessities for forces, attractions, etc., which are only necessities for verbs in certain other positions and so on.

We developed a particlelike description of the world because our language needed nouns. Now that the formulation of the world in particle and force terms has proved clumsy and inadequate, we have invented fields which blend the older separate "particles" and "forces" together into unified wholes.

Although it may be easy to use the notion of fields in place of discrete subatomic particles, it is more difficult to use these ideas in restructuring our views about ordinary objects in our everyday world. We are accustomed to seeing ordinary objects of our world and working with them as if they were just that—solid, discrete objects with definite boundaries, limited extension, and little influence. We can, however, perceive every ordinary object in much broader terms.

Pick up some simple object and examine it. Quietly touch it all over with your eyes closed. Then look at it. Try to be internally silent.

Now write down as many uses and functions of the object as you can think of. Write down the origins of the object and something about the people and skills that have gone into

bringing this particular object into your hands in its present form. How many years of evolution, of growth, of development went into the materials that comprise this object? What are some of the probable future dispositions of the object? In other words try to obtain a picture of the set of world lines for this simple object. And then blur your world line picture into a field picture. First consider the field (a five-dimensional one) surrounding the object. What are its interactions with other objects, with yourself and with other people? Can you come to a point of view in which the object is not a discrete, solitary entity, but merely a central region of a five-demensional field that extends to the limits of your perception in all directions, interacting with nearly all the things and events in the entire world? How big is one simple object! Try to see other objects in this manner.

After a short while you can almost automatically sense the bigness of every object in your environment. As you become used to thinking-perceiving in this fashion you will find the world much broader and more independent than you had previously thought. Einstein's thinking makes these relationships even more self-evident. Again, take in your hand any nearby, convenient physical object. The mere act of moving your hand involves space and time both. In fact, we define motion as the ratio between the two. The piece of matter which you may be holding before you is not purely an isolated piece of "matter." It necessarily takes up some space. In picking up the matter you have also picked up some space. As a bit of matter-space, the object which you hold in your hand exists—i.e., it must endure in time. Time is necessarily involved if space is. And so is energy, for Einstein showed that any bit of matter was equivalent to a gob of energy. His relationship between matter and energy, $E = mc^2$, involves space and time as well for "c" represents the velocity of light which is a ratio of a space interval to a time interval.

Furthermore, your object also has some definite form or

structure, some shape or organized pattern, even if it is as "formless" as water. All of these properties are not independent; each is a part of a whole, interrelated and necessary for the existence of the whole. We have an indivisible oneness: matter-energy-space-time-form.

Since science and our language has split this "oneness" into separate parts called space, time, energy, form, and matter, we have distorted their true relationship. Even where science has acknowledged the "oneness," the old conception still remains rooted in our speech and our minds.

Going a step further, we must ask if any chunk of the universe can be said to exist without someone's having touched it, weighed it, perceived its shape and its existence in time. We may talk about it, we may infer its existence but we cannot definitely know it until we have observed it or its manifestations. This was Einstein's other contribution: that we must take into account our perception and our means of measurement if we are to speak meaningfully about the universe. It follows, then, that we must be aware not only of the mechanical apparatus with which we measure the universe but also of the biases, distortions, and limitations of our own perceptual apparatus, our cognition processes, and, ultimately, our consciousness.*

Although science had redefined its terms and partially integrated the fragmented universe, we have not made this integration in our understanding or in our use of language. Perhaps you have begun to see how subtly words shape and distort our view of the universe. With words we can split the universe into parts; but when we do so, our senses tell us that we

*Perhaps you can recognize some similarity between this notion of modern physics which takes the observer into account and the two aspects of consciousness discussed in Chapter III; perception of the external world and awareness of yourself as being in the world.

lie. Although the theory of relativity is an accepted fact now, our everyday language still holds on to the old meanings; we cleave to static notions of a separate "time," "space," "matter," "energy," and to a queer abstraction called "form," all independent of a real human observer.

We don't usually perceive the "depths" of objects or the interrelatedness of things for three reasons: (1) the biological limitations of our sensing organs, (2) our weakly developed time-consciousness which perceives only the short-term nowness of events, and (3) our inherited language which artificially carves the world into discrete units and elements.

I have discussed the biological limitations of our sensing organs in Chapter II and our time-consciousness in Part 2. In this chapter I have briefly suggested that our language restricts our perception of things and events and makes it harder for us to make peace with a field view of the world. Let's pursue this point a bit further.

Because we are given prepared categories of language, we find it easy to carve up physical reality into little pieces—pieces of space, pieces of time, pieces of events (like causes and effects), and so on. We can *talk* about a *piece* of wood, the *foot* of a mountain, the *end* of a stick, or *empty space,* yet such objects do not exist in isolation. We cannot have the end of a stick without having the stick itself. Any piece of wood must have some definite shape, and the foot of the mountain blends imperceptibly into the edge of the valley. Obviously, there is no such thing as "emptiness" or pure "space." These are convenient abstractions, not physical realities. However, because we have discrete, distinct terms in our language we sometimes fall into the habit of thinking that there exist correspondingly discrete distinct physical things. (After all, we have been told that a noun is a person, place, or thing.)

Whorf points out that we cut up nature with our words and that we are all party to an agreement as to how it should be cut —though this agreement is unstated. We accept the agreement as we learn the language; no individual escapes this constraint. Language thinks for us and bounds our creative expression. Perhaps this is why new thoughts so often require new words. Ordinarily, the use of our language to cut up nature into chunks does not present any great difficulties. It is only when we push into new territory that we must guard against the traps of language.

The field notions of modern physics could not arise until some of these linguistic splits had been healed. As long as an older, antiquated, elementalistic language was in use, physicists were restricted in their understanding of the world. Now physicists have begun to recognize that "matter," "energy," "space," and "time" are only separate linguistic entities and that underneath them lies a single event-process or "field." Different kinds of distortions of this field lead to different manifestations—i.e., electric, magnetic, gravitational, or particulate—each with the property called energy which allows interactions with other kinks or distortions of the basic field.

Unfortunately, we still think of human beings as separate individuals, a viewpoint as inadequate and limited as our former conceptions of electrons as discrete particles. What, after all is an individual? Can an individual exist without a group? Without a mama and a papa? No. You and I, like electrons, have meaning and value only in context. The importance of a person includes not merely his physical body, but his interactions with the rest of humanity. His being and his happening are as inseparable as electrons and their electromagnetic-gravitational fields. Only the words are separate.

If we look around we see that everyone is connected, in fact almost defined, by interactions with other people. How can there be a teacher without students, a businessman without customers, or a lover without a beloved? There are hermits 'tis true, but not self-propagating ones.

Every man belongs to many communities. These communities —Presbyterian, storekeeper, Democrat, skier, Mason, stockholder —may overlap in complex patterns of purposes and interests just as psychological events run parallel to and overlap each other.

A girl in Seattle belongs to countless associations, local and universal; as she puts on her lipstick she enters indirectly into an economic pattern which embraces men and organizations throughout the world. Her breakfast, if she has one, is an international feast, of coffee from Brazil, sugar from Hawaii, orange juice from Florida, eggs from Montana, bacon from Canada, toast of wheat from over the mountains, marmalade from California, and chemicals from the bowels of the earth. Her radio may accompany her with an African rhythm, her spoon comes from Sweden, her pottery bowl from a hippie commune in Vermont. The electric trolley she takes to the office is the work of countless men from ages past and present; of Volta, Stephenson, Faraday, Maxwell, of miners, seamen, ticket punchers, and millions more.

> We all, in brief, live in and by miracles of community and collaboration. We belong to communities and societies whose threads are woven into the whole pattern of the world since its beginnings. This complex of common interest and purposes and acts and ideas is the most massive fact of man's existence as a social being. Yet it is one of the most neglected in our daily concern with the world.*

Probably no more literal and vivid example of the interconnectedness of people exists than mountaineers who must

*Paul McGuire, "The Human Community," in *A Collection of Readings for Writers,* edited by H. Shaw.

tie themselves to each other with a rope. If one falls, the others are endangered. The very life of each man relates directly to the actions of the other men on the rope.

More subtle human interconnections have been exposed in the last twenty years or so in the field of mental health. Most psychiatrists now recognize that if one member of a family suffers from an illness, other members of the family are unavoidably involved in that illness. Trigant Burrow, Wilhelm Reich, Harold Searles and other psychiatrists say that our entire culture is sick and no one individual can be wholly cured until we are all cured. This represents a big advance over earlier notions of treating either "bodies" or "minds" as though they were separate entities.

Not only do all men interrelate with each other, but they also relate to other organisms in a very real sense. Consider the foods we eat. These foods, which were once living things—parts of plants and animals, cells, seeds, eggs, tissues—all literally become part of our physical bodies. In turn, our bodies excrete wastes that are foods for other animals and microorganisms. When we die, our bodies become food for bacteria, and even as we live, some bacteria feed upon us, helping us digest other food. Each living organism eats and is eaten—each shares its life-matter-energy in many ways with other living organisms. There are specialized protozoa which inhabit the gut of the termite; each termite clan passes on its own special strain of protozoa to its descendants, as if it was the sacred torch of its existence and indeed it is; separated, both termites and protozoa will die. There are the ant nations with their mushroom gardens. Whole forests live because of fungi which bridge the gap between soil-foods and their roots. There are the pollinators, insects usually, which fertilize the seeds of plant and tree in return for their own special foods. There are the almost "social" associations, like those between the shark and the pilot fish, the rhinoceros and the tickbird, associations in which mutual services are responsibly rendered. And there are little fish which clean the teeth of big fish.

After writing these words I waded out in the sea and perched on a seaweed-covered rock to relax. When I looked closely at the big weeds on the rock, I saw fine fluffy seaweeds of an entirely different type growing right on the bigger weeds.

In these fluffy seaweeds little clam seedlings had their start, more secure there than on sand or bare rock. Tiny white worms crawled busily around in the fluffy seaweed. Lifting up the thick, ropy masses of primary seaweed I discovered a dozen tiny starfish busily working at their own molasses-like pace. Scattered amongst the starfish innumerable snails hid in safety, enclosed in their hard shells. The longer I looked the more life I saw. Each species can only exist on that rock in the sea if the others also exist. Each shares, eats and is eaten, lives, and dies in intimate connection with the whole. Even inorganic things partake in this mutual feast. The primary seaweed needs the rock to anchor on, and the seaweeds protect the rocks from eroding rapidly away (by rock time) in the sea's currents.

Instead of looking at the human body as a fixed object we can see it as a focal point in a complex food cycle. Viewed as an organic process, the body represents a nexus in a flowing stream of proteins, carbohydrates, minerals, and vitamins derived from other organisms, which, in their turn, were nexuses of flowing streams of material from other organisms, materials, or sun energy. In an ever-widening cycle our bodies are ultimately connected with everything in the universe. Who can say exactly where you end and I begin? As Walter Harrison wrote:

> The more widely we look and the more completely we see, the more intricate and all-embracing is the linkage displayed before us and which unites, not only all forms of life, but matter no less. It has been said that if a man raises a finger he creates a corresponding, albeit infinitesimal, displacement in the stars, such is the absolute and all

extending link between everything that is. On the same terms to kill a wood-louse, pluck a leaf, or cut a blade of grass must send an infinitesimal quiver through all living things.*

We came to believe that the universe consists of separate, independent parts, but this has not proved justifiable in the world of elementary particles, in the world of psychology, or on our planet earth with its growing pollution problems. Alan Watts writes:

Suns, stars, and planets provide the conditions in which and from which organisms can arise. Their peculiar structure *implies* organisms in such a way that, were there no organisms, the structure of the universe would be entirely different, and so that organisms in their turn, imply a universe of just this structure. It is only the time lag and the immense complexity of the relations between stars and men which make it difficult to see that they imply one another just as much as men and women, or the two poles of the earth. As a tree produces leaves, so the universe peoples.†

We have lost our conception of ourselves as part of a cultural whole—perhaps because most of us live a schizophrenic-like existence in our cocoons of steel, glass, plastic, and concrete, with our air filtered, our shades drawn, and our heads filled with words and symbols.

Indians such as the Wentu, who live much closer to the natural world, regard each individual person as an instantiation of "man," like fingers to the hand—separate, but part of the whole. Maybe this next exercise will bring you back to this view.

To expand your perception, do with another person what you did with objects. Look at a particular person. Try to perceive that person in his seeming here-now existence as a focal point for streams of organic life. Try to perceive that person as a focal point for many interactions—psychological, social, cultural.

* *The Threshold of Discovery*, pp. 49–50.
† *Nature, Man, and Woman*, p. 176.

Consider his roles, functions, activities as world lines. How big is he? How is he connected with you and your network of world lines? With the physical, natural environment around him? Then integrate the world-line model into a field model. Can you imagine a person as merely the particulate point of a five-dimensional field? Look into his eyes and through them into the field which surrounds him and from which his existence springs.

We limit our perception of the field aspects of others and ourselves by our prescientific habits of thinking. When we can transcend these limitations by knowledge gained from extraneural means of perception (microscopes, voltmeters, spectrometers, and so forth) integrating the knowledge with our modern scientific ways of thinking, or when we can transcend these limitations by blocking random thought through the attainment of inner silence, then we come to a fuller view of man.

If we look at events as something more like fields, focal points of energy, or informational flow patterns, and if we attend more to the wholeness of the field rather than the individual points within the field we will find our lives—and our consciousness—expanding enormously. As I eat, I look at the candles on the table. But candles are not just candles, they are the products of labor, they were purchased on Cape Cod, during a vacation trip. They are beautiful shapes, rich in colors, design, and craftsmanship, the evolved product of thousands of years of human efforts.

As I sit with my friend and talk, I sense so much more than his mere physical prescence. Through him shine all the years of his life, his joys, his sufferings, his hopes, his future plans. All of this and more is there if I just look with my higher mind's eye.

Let's explore one other aspect in our developing picture of man as a field. This time we will take as our starting point information rather than energy.

Suppose that you are a creature from another planet whose mode of perception consists only of being sensitive to information, regardless of the energy channel in which it presents itself. How would you see a man? Certainly not as a physical body, but rather as a source of information. Information can be thought of as patterns of energy change. For example, when we speak we produce pressure changes in the air. This requires energy; but it is the pattern of the energy that is important. The pattern, transmitted as pressure changes, conveys information. The pattern remains invariant, even though we can transcribe the air-density changes into an electrical signal, transmit them over telephone wires, or via electromagnetic waves, or even store them on magnetic tape. The basic energy carrier differs in each case, but the information, which is the essence of the message, remains approximately the same. If you, as an alien being, are sensitive only to information, including of course that information conveyed by ink marks on paper, you would see human beings as sources, emitting and receiving vast quantities of information. You would have an entirely different concept of the "size" of a human being, for a person would be as big as his radiated information field. A single person could fill the globe. He can phone across the country in an instant. He can write letters anywhere in the world. He can appear on TV relayed by satellite across an ocean and his infomation pattern can be radiated to millions of other people.

Moreover, a single individual's information pattern transcends the personal life of his organism. I have written this book and you may read it long after my physical body dies. The only interaction between you and I is via the information—patterns of ink on a page.

The information field of a human does not follow the same laws of time as physical bodies, nor is there the same separateness which we have grown accustomed to accept. When you perceive people as fields of information, sharp boundaries between one person and another fade away. The patterns of information in this book are woven together from many sources. What I have written you may read and write or speak about to someone else who may add to it and pass it on to others. Each human source of information is like a ripple from a pebble thrown into the water that spreads out and blends with other ripples. I cannot say what thoughts are uniquely mine when I write or speak. Through me flow the ideas of men from centuries ago as well as those of yesterday. Neither time nor space separates me from them and me from you at the information level. Ideas have their own life and their own existence, independent of the physical organisms which store and transmit them.

There are about three billion people on the earth. They amount to about a million tons of neural cortex for storing information—information which is shared, modified, recorded, or stored by extra neural means such as books, photographs, tapes, etc., and transmitted from language to language, from parent to child, from culture to culture, from century to century in a never-ending process. A vast shuffling, dancing, mixing, and blending of information covers the whole earth like clouds of water vapor that form and mix, swirl and dissipate in the air only to reappear elsewhere in some other form. If we could only see this as our mythical alien creature might! What a picture of humanity!

In the information field, as in the material realm, each person is a blend of others. Each person with whom you connect weaves his own information field into yours to some degree. Everyone is informationally mixed up with everyone else on the earth. The resulting social tapestry constitutes the superorganism or noosphere described by Teilhard de Chardin. Woven from humanity's informational threads, the noosphere extends millions of years back.

Even at the level of ordinary consciousness, we are not separate. We think of man as an independent, autonomous creature partly because language has given us the little word "I," and it leads us to assume that we function as separate beings.* This concept is very far from the truth. Because we assume that we are unique, solitary, autonomous individuals, we think each person should be responsible for his own actions, behavior, and morals. We have trouble identifying with others or understanding their points of view. We teach our children to be competitive rather than cooperative, to be self-sufficient, independent, strong, and egotistic. All of our social institutions are built upon the premise that men operate as individuals. As Watts wrote:

> . . . is it not obvious that what may start out as a small and unnoticed mistake may turn into a catastrophe as one rolling pebble may start an avalanche? Who could have known that the mistake of regarding men as separate egos would have had such disastrous consequences?†

All the facts at all levels cry out our universal relationship with all things. Our education, our "i's," and our social structure have split us and keep us from uniting with ourselves, with each other, and with the world. If we are to fulfill and preserve ourselves, we must strive to break down every kind of barrier that prevents separate beings from uniting. Instead of saying "I Love You," it would be more accurate to say "We love us."

From the field point of view, we are not separate from one another or from the universe which spawned us, but are instead multidimensional beings consisting of complex knots of organic

*Not all languages and cultures have been so tied to the pronoun "I." For example, the Javanese commonly refers to a spouse as "I" and to the spouse's property, activities, and even opinions as "mine." Use of I in this way orients the Javanese toward viewing events from their spouse's perspective much better than we would be able to do. It may also lead him to a much greater awareness of the other's individuality within his own personality, and intensify his emotional ties. (Robert Jay, *Javanese Villagers*. M.I.T. Press, 1968)
† *Psychotherapy East and West.* Jonathan Cape, 1971 (p. 124).

fields, patterned structures of proteins, fats, carbohydrates, and minerals connected to the vegetable and animal kingdoms. As carriers of information we share the knowledge of the whole world, its customs, roles, rituals, and behaviors. Our living and choosing form parts of fields (defined by world lines in psychological event-space) that transcend space-time, extending to all the realities that were, are, might have been, or will be. We extend in all directions, into all dimensions and are all interconnected. The We-Field comprises the entire universe in one whole.

Although this may seem a bizarre or "far out" notion it carries more validity than the viewpoint held by most people. We cannot separate ourselves from our world or from each other any more than time, space, matter, energy, form, and consciousness can be split asunder. Mind and universe are as inseparable as front and back.

From these considerations the "oneness" of the universe emerges as a scientific fact. There is no need to use the term "mystical" for something so obvious and straightforward. When you understand this viscerally, you will understand how all men may be called brothers and that the golden rule: "Do unto thy neighbor as to thyself" is no arbitrary prescription, but arises quite logically from the fact that you are inextricably connected with your neighbor.

You will get a more direct experience of this as you try the final exercise. Get together with a few friends and sit in a circle facing each other and holding hands:

Begin by focusing your attention on your own physical body. Close your eyes. Systematically let your attention rove from your scalp to your eyes, nose, cheeks, ears, mouth, chin, neck, back of neck, etc. Work your way slowly through your entire body, letting your attention change from point to point like a searchlight, going into your arms, fingers, returning, going to your

legs, feet, returning, etc. Center your attention at the solar plexus, then move it out one arm and into the fingers, hand, arm, etc. of the person to one side of you. Travel within their body as you did your own, then return and move into the body of the person next to you. See how far you can move around the circle; see how much of the we-field you can take in. Open your eyes, maintain eye contact and continue letting your attention move within the others in the circle. Expand your consciousness—let it flow into a field.

"Why do you love people?" asked the disciple.
"What else can I do?" replied the master.

XIII

Life and Death and Life and Death and Life . . .

"Did you say 'pig', or 'fig'?" said the Cat.

"I said 'pig'," replied Alice; "and I wish you wouldn't keep appearing and vanishing so suddenly: you make one quite giddy!"

"All right," said the Cat; and this time it vanished quite slowly, beginning with the end of the tail, and ending with the grin, which remained some time after the rest of it had gone.

"Well! I've often seen a cat without a grin," thought Alice; "but a grin without a cat! It's the most curious thing I ever saw in all my life!"

—LEWIS CARROLL

It's as improbable to be born once as it is to be born twice.

—Zen teacher

A cabbage differs from a king only in the arrangement of its energy patterns, as anything differs from any other thing because of its organization or patternment, not because it is made of a different material or substance. Relationships between elements are more important than the elements themselves. The structure of a thing or an event determines its uniqueness. The split between matter and form, like that between space and time, should never have been allowed to persist for two thousand years in our language or our thinking. Everywhere we look we see that the richness and variety of things result from their form, their ordered structure, and not to any difference in elemental materials. The various forms of water delight us and enrich the earth: blue-green ocean water; emerald pools; wispy, fluffy, or angry clouds; sparkling icicles; singing brooks; and crashing waves. Looking at a book of photographs of snow crystals stills the mind with awe and wonder at nature's endless creativity. Coal, lampblack, graphite, charcoal, and diamonds are markedly different structures of the same element—carbon—and they have vastly different properties and uses. We burn coal for warmth treat charcoal as garbage, write with graphite pencil "leads", and fight over diamonds.

We are different from each other because our structures are different. Indeed, structure is the key to life. Apes and monkeys resemble humans and possess approximately the same distribution of basic elements but their nervous system, and physiology is considerably less complex.

Our bodies consist mainly of carbon, hydrogen, nitrogen, and oxygen atoms. Yet these atoms do not combine in random, haphazard clumps but in highly structured, tremendously complex organizations, interlaced with a sprinkling of about seventy other kinds of atoms. It is this complex structure that makes our bodies capable of being and achieving so much. Tossed in an unorganized heap, the pile of chemicals making up a human body would not impress us much, but put together in a way that is elusively beyond our grasp, we have the miracle of life.

If we carry our analysis deeper, we also find that carbon, hydrogen, oxygen, and other atoms differ only in their structure and not because of any intrinsic properties or unique subatomic particles. Each kind of atom differs from others only in the number and arrangement of electrons, protons, and neutrons of which it is composed. Hydrogen, the simplest, consists of one electron and one proton; carbon, of fourteen of each, plus fourteen neutrons; oxygen of sixteen each plus sixteen neutrons.

Moreover, as we discussed earlier, electrons, protons, and neutrons are merely names for places where space-time arranges itself in a definite fashion. At the very smallest level we are all simply structured patterns of space-time-energy. And it therefore follows that we must exist in a fifth dimension—physically as well as psychologically. I am one five-dimensional pattern and you are another.

How does it happen that the patterns we call ourselves become manifest as physical organisms? What is it that arranges your structure and my structure and everybody's and everything's structure in their unique fashion?

The physical body arises largely from master patterns present in the genes. Just as information is bound in books and stored in libraries for man's later use, so information is biologically bound in genes and transmitted from parent to child. The genetic code carried by DNA and RNA molecules provides the pattern, the blueprint, that directs the growth of my body and yours. In fact, each cell of your current body is only about the fiftieth or sixtieth descendant of the egg at conception. Furthermore, nearly every cell in your body carries *two* copies of the genetic code that was present in the original egg cell. The information stored in your gene cells passes to your children; it is the biological you and, as a pattern, it transcends the life and death of your physical body.

Death is a queer sort of thing that happens only to living organisms that have developed fixed body forms. Organisms which reproduce by splitting in two, such as fungus, amoeba, bacteria, or jellyfish, never die! Only organisms that reproduce sexually die individual deaths, though the product of the fusion of the two entities (children) lives on. The basic genetic patterns flow down a lifeline of descendants through mothers, fathers, brothers, cousins, and so on.

Can you visualize drawing a set of world lines of gene patterns for generation after generation? Living organisms are just carriers of gene patterns, as records are carriers of music—the individual record may come and go but the music exists indefinitely. Gene patterns, too, flow from one organism to another, mixing, blending, fusing, but never wholly ceasing to exist. A single isolated organism is just one representation of some genetic information at one space-time region—a particular conjunction of intersecting fields. Everyone is genetically related to everyone else. We all form links in a chain reaction of genetic events that surpasses the human imagination.

Perhaps it is more like a five-dimensional tapestry, where our organisms hang like pearls on threads. Our individual bodies come and go out of existence as the genetic threads weave through them. Thousands of threads twist into each pearl of consciousness and flow on to other pearls. Sometimes, in our ignorance, we naïvely believe that we are the pearls; but we are more than that for we are connected with the whole tapestry of living organisms, itself a design on a background of all nonliving matter-fields as well. All the pearls are woven together in some master design beyond the ken of ordinary consciousness. At the deepest physical level, as well as at the level of higher consciousness, only a flowing connectedness exists, a we-field of thee and me and everyone and everything.

Who am I?
Who are You?
Who are We?
Patterns within Patterns
Within Patterns

By Involution, Evolution, Revolution
The many return into the One.

Who are we indeed? We are patterns, but what kind of patterns? Of what? At which level? Where am I to find myself amidst all these swirling, whirling, mixing patterns and patterns of patterns? Which one am I to identify with? Which is the real me?

Let's sort them out a bit more analytically.

At least four components can be distinguished among the patterned energy fields which come into focus as our organisms: the chemical, the physical, the psychosocial, and the ones comprising essence.

The arrangements of subatomic particles into elements and the formation of these elements into chemical compounds is provided for us ready-made for the most part. The earth already contains the elements and most of the basic chemicals needed for existence, save for a few which our bodies make internally.

The patterns of our physical structure—the cells, bones, tissues, and organs—are organized by meta-patterns stored in the genes that direct our construction from the streams of organic foods and chemicals which flow through us.

While our physical structure is growing, we acquire external patterns, superimposed upon us by psychological, social, cultural, and semantic environments. Those patterns may alter our physical structure, e.g., you may decide to become an athlete and hence develop your body. Or you may become traumatized by fears and inhibitions which block the full growth of your body, and alter its chemistry. You may acquire a job such as a copy writer, or jeweler, or carpenter which subtly shapes your body over the years. The external patterns, the "forces" that shape the body's physical growth and muscular formation, constitute the physical component of the acquired personality.

The physical shape of our bodies is also modified by the stresses of living.

The psychosocial patterns of our acquired personalities, beliefs, attitudes, ideas, ways of feeling, thinking, or behaving, are acquired from parents, teachers, peers, and the media of books, newspapers, movies, television, etc. The personal consciousness of ordinary everyday life is simply a patterned knot in an information net that today, with our modern technology of communication, is rapidly expanding to include the entire human race on earth.

Behind the acquired set of psychosocial patterns lie the meta-patterns which constitute essence. Just as the genetic master-patterns direct the construction of our physical bodies, the meta-patterns of essence guide our psychological growth and formation even though they are often overwhelmed or strongly distorted by the influences of the world. I believe, but I cannot prove, that essence-patterns transcend the life and death of our physical organisms and our individually acquired personalities, just as do gene-patterns.

Essence makes up the eternal component of us, the five-dimensional patterns which live through our four-dimensional bodies and often break through our acquired personalities into our ordinary four-dimensional consciousness. By meditating, being here-now, training our brain waves, or otherwise disidentifying with our acquired personalities, we may allow essence freer expression and guidance of our lives. Essence is not some mystical *élan vital,* it is a meta-pattern of information superimposed upon the coarser matter of our visible world. It is our inner core, our inner sparkle of joy and life.

Perhaps, after all, essence is only our smile, like the cat's grin —all the rest being mere embroidery.

Formulating essence as a meta-pattern, although not yet demonstrable by modern scientific inference, provides a logical basis for life after death and the occurrence of successive reincarnations, for a pattern can exist independently of the material which manifests it. Just as a musical score may exist as black, patterned marks on lined paper, as wiggles in a phonograph record, or as magnetized spots on a tape, so essence seems to exist independently of physical bodies.

When music is transmitted as radio waves, radios and speakers are needed to transform it into perceptible sound, but it still exists whether or not those radios are operating. So, too, we may need musical instruments to perform a symphony, but the music may exist in unmanifest form indefinitely. As a pattern imprinted on some medium, music transcends the life and death of individual performances, conductors, radios, speakers, and even listeners. Analogously, we have electronic circuit diagrams and rules for making instruments such as radios, TVs, amplifiers, and so on. The circuits are manifested or brought into actuality by putting the physical parts together. We have blueprints for making a house, mathematical formulae for designing airplane wings, boat hulls, light bulbs, etc., or simply prose directions for making shoes and sealing wax. The patterns, as organizing rules, can exist in many different mediums. Only the actualities are restricted.

Science does not yet know the medium in which essence is the message. Perhaps essence patterns exist all around us, invisible, waiting to become manifest like the radio waves that imperceptibly bathe us, unseen and unheard until we turn on the TV and tune it to the proper channel.

Physical bodies and personalities serve as the instruments through which essence plays its finer music. Although we naïvely think we are our bodies, we really only use them for a short while. The body seems to be the amplifier for the brain and the brain the amplifier for essence and higher consciousness. We are so much more than the mere corporeal organism, so much more than a bag of skin and bones holding blood and nerves and muscles together. If one amplifier is destroyed or gradually weakens and finally dies, we merely pick another one.

Life is our biggest hang-up.

As an essence pattern we live through our bodies, in symbiosis but not in absolute control over them. Essence flows into and out of our physical bodies as they are born and die—just as streams of foods, genetic patterns, or psychosocial personality patterns flow into specific individuals, dissolve, and pass on in other forms.

From a four-dimensional view, essence pops in and out of body world lines like neural impulses jumping between synaptic connections in the brain. Essence may be manifest in one body for some clock time, permeating the coarser matter of cells and tissues, but when that one body is turned off, essence moves on, becoming manifest in another physical body at another point in time (or space).

We do not know exactly how this transfer of information, this essence pattern, comes to manifest itself in the organism, or how it transfers from one body to another in the time dimension. The pattern definitely does transfer, however. Memories of another existence flicker through our lives, suddenly coming to awareness now and then, gaps in the fabric of time, glimpses from transcendental moments into elsewhen, fading away in the rush of the present moment.

Usually only the vaguest and weakest impressions tunnel through the barriers from one time-consciousness to another. Perhaps only those few instances when we are fully here-now in the most intense fashion penetrate the cloak of personality to make their mark on the meta-patterns of essence and become carried over into its other manifestations.

From a field viewpoint, essence may be only temporarily focused in one body, and no more limited to a single body in a single space-time region any more than a radio broadcast is limited to one receiving set at a time. Not only may the same essence patterns reincarnate or manifest themselves at different points along the lifelines of living organisms, but they may reoccur in several (or perhaps hundreds) of different physical bodies at the same time level.

Perhaps human sexuality involves more than the mere physical attraction between male and female—more than the seeking of a physical organism to complete itself and to avoid death by reproducing gene patterns. Perhaps at a different level sexual intercourse may tie together related essence patterns locked into their separate physical bodies and covered over by outer personalities. At its deepest level, is love merely essence seeking its own, weaving its own tapestry in a five-dimensional universe of all living beings that ever were, are, and will be? And what pattern, what kind of higher consciousness lies beyond essence that plays its part, however weakly in our lives?

Who knows?
You know . . . .
You can get there . . . .
You are there
here . . .
now. . . .
Always.

| XIV |

Where Are We?

Before you have studied Zen, mountains are mountains and
rivers are rivers. While you are studying Zen, mountains are
not mountains and rivers are not rivers. After you have
studied Zen, mountains are mountains and rivers are rivers.

In this book I've led you very far away, sometimes plunging into
abstract physics, into the complicated world of subatomic
particles, or the chemistry and neurology of the body. There are
so many words and so much to think about. But after all this, the
expansion and evolution of consciousness is a simple enough
process—only sometimes we have to go the long way around.
Perhaps it is like climbing a mountain. As every mountain climber
knows, being on the summit is not the real meaning of the climb.
Once there, at the peak, one can only return. The vital core of
the experience lies in the journey itself. That is why an airplane
trip over the mountains or a ride to a summit in a cable car is
never as satisfying as climbing by one's own willful efforts. The
view may be beautiful and you may obtain some guidelines for
your climbs, but the airplane can never replace the actual
climbing experience. Man sets his goals so he can make his
journeys.

Perhaps the thoughts in this book will help you set some goals and begin some journeys. The exercises are starting points, but the real work is up to you. Ultimately no one can help you if you don't want to be helped. My way may not be your way. Each person starts at a different place in his evolutionary journey and each may have his own mountain to climb or his own route to the summit. May your trip be fruitful and fulfilling.

When you return you will see that you didn't really have to go. Everything is here just as it should be. There is nothing to be done differently except to be aware. The end point is the same as the beginning. When you are there and done you will really see that you're just right here eating a banana, reading a book, or cleaning the refrigerator. Where else could you be! Getting "there" is only getting "here," after all.

Barefooted and naked of breast, I mingle with the people of the world.
My clothes are ragged and dust-laden, and I am ever blissful.
I use no magic to extend my life;
Now, before me, the dead trees become alive.

—Tenth Zen Bull, Zen Flesh, Zen Bones

RETURN

A little too abstract, a little too wise,
It is time for us to kiss the earth again,
It is time for us to let the leaves rain from the skies,
Let the rich life run to the roots again.
I will go down to the lovely Sur Rivers
And dip my arms in them up to the shoulders. . . .

I will touch things and things and no more thoughts. . . .
        noble is the mountain,
         Oh noble
Pico Blanco, steep sea-wave of marble.

—ROBINSON JEFFERS

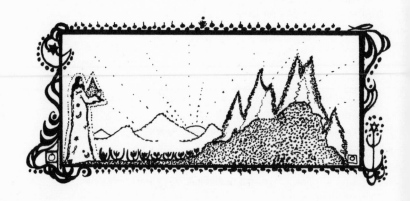

Additional References

These works are listed in the order of their importance to me, and are followed by a few selected reference books.

Science and Sanity, Alfred Korzybski, Non-Aristotelian Publishing Co., 1933.
In Search of the Miraculous; Fragments of an Unknown Teaching, P. D. Ouspensky. Routledge & Kegan Paul, 1950.
Gestalt Therapy, Frederick S. Perls, Ralph F. Hefferline, and Paul Goodman. Julian Press, 1951.
Language, Thought, and Reality, Benjamin Lee Whorf. M.I.T. Press, 1956.
Zen Flesh, Zen Bones, Paul Reps. Doubleday Anchor Books, 1961.
The Books of Charles Fort, Charles Fort. Henry Holt, 1941.
Psychological Commentaries on the Teachings of G. I. Gurdjieff and P. D. Ouspensky, M. Nicoll. Vincent Stuart Ltd., 1952.
The Fourth Way, P. D. Ouspensky. Knopf, 1965.
All and Everything, G. Gurdjieff. E. P. Dutton, 1964.
Meetings with Remarkable Men, G. Gurdjieff. Routledge & Kegan Paul, 1963.
The Book: On the Taboo against Knowing Who You Are, Alan W. Watts. Jonathan Cape, 1969.
The Betty Book, Stewart E. White. Robert Hale, 1945.
The Process, Brion Gysin. Doubleday, 1963.
"I Looked Up", The Incredible String Band, Electra Records, EKS-74061, 1970.
The Phenomenon of Man, Pierre Teilhard de Chardin. Harper, 1959.
The Future of Man, Pierre Teilhard de Chardin. Collins, 1964.
The Joyous Cosmology, Alan W. Watts. Pantheon, 1962.
Psychological Excercises and Essays, Alfred R. Orage. The Janus Press, 1965.
The Upanishads, Swami Prabhavananda and Frederick Manchester, translators. New American Library, 1948.
The Master Game, Robert S. DeRopp. Allen & Unwin, 1969.
You Are Not the Target, Laura Huxley. Heinemann, 1964.
The Supreme Doctrine, Hubert Benoit. Routledge & Kegan Paul, 1955.

The Sufis, Idries Shah. W. H. Allen, 1964.
Commentaries on Living, Jiddu Krishnamurti. Quest Books, 1956.

GENERAL REFERENCES

The World of Elementary Particles, Kenneth Ford. Blaisdell Press, 1963.
The Voices of Time, Julius T. Fraser, ed. Braziller, 1965.
"Hypnotic Alterations of Space and Time," Bernard Aaronson. *International Journal of Parapsychology,* Vol. X, No. 1, 1968.
George Ellett Coghill, Charles J. Herrick. University of Chicago Press, 1949.
Flatland: A Romance of Many Dimensions, Edwin A. Abbot. Barnes and Noble, 1963.
The Universe and Doctor Einstein, Lincoln K. Barnett. Victor Gollancz, 1949.
Hidden Channels of the Mind, Louisa E. Rhine. Victor Gollancz, 1962.

REFERENCES ON BIOFEEDBACK, MEDITATION, AND INSTRUMENTATION

PsychoPhysics Labs, Inc., 31 Townsend Terrace, Framingham, Mass. 01760
Biofeedback Instruments, 213 West Plain Street, Wayland, Mass. 01778
The Greatest Power in the Universe, Uell S. Andersen, Atlantis University, 1971.
Biofeedback–Turning on the power of your mind, M. Karlins and L. M. Andrews, Garnstone Press, London, 1973.
For a comprehensive bibliography of meditation research write to:

> Meditation Research Information Exchange
> Beverly Timmons, Coordinator
> Langley Porter Institute
> 401 Parnassus Avenue
> San Francisco, Calif. 94122

For information about the Biofeedback Society write to:

> The Secretary, Ms Francine Butler
> Department of Psychiatry
> Room 202, University of Colorado Medical Centre
> 4200 East Ninth Avenue
> Denver, Colo. 80220

For collected readings of many of the above titles and other publications see:
Biofeedback and Self-Control: 1970, An Aldine Annual on the Regulation of Bodily Processes and Consciousness, Theodore X. Barber *et al.*
Biofeedback and Self-Control: 1971, An Aldine Annual on the Regulation of Bodily Processes and Consciousness, Johann Stoyva *et al.*
Biofeedback and Self-Control: 1972, An Aldine Annual on the Regulation of Bodily Processes and Consciousness, David Shapiro *et al.*
Biofeedback and Self-Control: 1971, An Aldine Reader on the Regulation of Bodily Processes and Consciousness, Theodore X. Barber *et al.*

These books are available from Aleph One Ltd, P.O. Box 72, Cambridge CB3 0NX
(Cambridge 811679).

Also contact Aleph One Ltd, who are Dr Payne's licensees for Britain and Western
Europe, for details of instruments.